"Restoring Regions"

Apostle Detrick L. Gaskins

"**Restoring Regions**" is a training manual filled with practical principals designed to equip leaders and believers alike in the arts of regional restoration. As you turn the pages, a spiritual impartation to take back spiritually what naturally belongs to you will emerge and transform you. The fulfillment of the scripture Is. 58:12 "and they that shall be of thee shall build waste places thou shall raise up the foundations of many generations and thou shall be called The repairer of the breach, The restorer of paths to dwell in" will finally be a tangible manifestation, not just a long awaited expectation.

Restoring Regions
ISBN 978-0692414293
Copyright © 2005
Detrick L. Gaskins
Orlando, FL 32811

Editing & Layout Design by
Ruah Publishing
Orlando, FL.

Cover Design
LaRoyce Art & Ruah Publishing
laroyce@thelightanddarkseries.com
www.thelightanddarkseries.com

All rights reserved under International Copyright Law. Contents and or cover may not be reproduced in whole or in part in any for without the express written consent of the publisher. Unless otherwise indicated, all scriptural quotations are from the *King James Version* of the bible. Printed in the United States

DEDICATION

I dedicate this book to my Lord and Savior Jesus Christ. I am so very proud of you and the work you are doing with me and the Body of Christ as a whole. Keep up the God work, I want to be just like you when I grow up. {Smiling}

I was also like to dedicate this manual to my daughter DeMeta Diani Gaskins You, along with the generations of leaders to follow, are the reason why I have penned this manual, that you might take the words herein and forward God's kingdom. Daddy loves you I declare God's continued provision, protection and prosperity over your life. May you walk in willingness and obedience to His plan for your life that you might feast on the good on the land.

SPECIAL THANKS

I'd like to give high honor and praise to the Gaskins, Edwards and Hardy families. To my 11 siblings, I love you with an undying love. To my mothers Doris v. Gaskins, and Little Irene Blackson, you both make me so proud to be called your son. Both of you have touched my life beyond words. May your lives be filled with God's longevity and blessings. To my father Levi Hardy, finding and meeting you was one of the finest moments of my life. I look forward to further developing our relationship, I love you.

Second, I would like to say a special thank you to Prophet Michael L. Hill, *Kingdom Life Ministries*, San Jose, California. For all the prophetic words that kept me on track and for all your silent and sometimes stern rebukes. Your support through the years as a friend and a co-laborer in the gospel has truly fulfilled the scripture, *there is a friend that sticks closer than a brother*. I speak strength and honor to your ministry, for truly you are a Prophet sent by God that shall be recognized in this end time.

Thirdly, I give special thanks to the Hill, Williams & Miller families. Your labors of love through, continued support and friendship has truly kept me going. You are the seeds that God planted to cause our ministry to grow. Thank you all for allowing God to use you, truly you are my apostleship in the Lord. I look forward to many more years of serving you. Love you much.

ACKNOWLEDGEMENTS

First, I would like to acknowledge God for giving me the grace to pen this manual. Without your insight, wisdom, correction and counsel this manual would be undone. Your much more than a son could ever desire in a Father. I pray that you would grant each reader *greater grace* and that restoration would flow through these pages impacting all who read and apply the principles therein.

Second, I would like to acknowledge Apostle Stephen Garner, *Rivers of Living Water International Ministries*, Chicago Il. Your life, teachings and continued support has truly touched my heart. Thanks for believing in the call of God upon my life. My prayer is that our fellowship and friendship would continue to grow and produce mighty rivers of restoring waters that will impact regions and generations to come. Thanks man of God, strength and honor to you.

I would also like to acknowledge all the partners of *KINSMEN Fellowship* for believing in me and adhering to the counsel of the Lord through me. To *Kairos International Training Center*, you have my heart. Thank you for supporting me as your overseer, friend and co-laborer. To my apostolic guard Apostle Ivory Hopkins, *Pilgrims Ministry of Deliverance, Georgetown, DE* thanks for looking out for me and allowing me to be apart of your apostolic canopy of believers. Your wisdom and knowledge as a general has been such a blessing to me and I honor you. I pray that God will strengthen our unity and continue to empower us to further God's house and His people through His spirit of restoration.

Apostle Detrick L. Gaskins

Book Layout

This book was designed for all believers, from the new born, to the adult Christian. Every appetite can be addressed. Each believer's spiritual appetite must be addressed differently and we pray that as you read this manual the hunger and thirst of your spirit will be filled.

Spiritual Appetite

Newborns
- Water: washes and sanctifies the believer. {Eph. 5:26}
- Milk: helps the spiritual growth {maturing}. {1 Pet. 2:2}

Adolescence
- Bread: gives us nourishment and deliverance. {Ex. 16; 1 Kin. 19:6-7; Matt. 6:11}

Adult
- Meat: gives us revelation, strength, substance, enlargement, advancement and endurance. {1 Kin. 19:6-8; Heb. 5:12-14}

Style of Writing

The authors style of writing can be simply deemed as a "Power Point Presentation"

Power: is the scriptures given within each chapter, section and topic within the book.
Point: represents each principle {revelation} extracted from the scripture. Keep in mind that all points given are not the only points that can be extracted from the particular scripture.
Presentation: is the **manifestation** of the Power and the Points as they are applied to the life of the believer and/or region.

Bible Friendly

This manual was designed for the reader to utilize their bible as they study. As you go through this manual each time you see the word READ you must pick up your bible and read the scriptures provided.

Manual Rating

This manual is rated **YA** for its ability to speak to YOUTH to the ADULT reader.

Note:
As you read and glean from this manual, please keep in mind that every region, nation, people, etc. are different. The contents of this manual are basic foundational techniques for *Regional Restoration*. Therefore, some points made may or may not apply in some instances. We admonish you to assess where you are, and be lead by the Holy Spirit before, and as you go forth in applying these principles or any other form of spiritual warfare.

PRE-THOUGHT

THE SPIRITUAL INSIGHT COMING FROM APOSTLE DETRICK L. GASKINS I FIND TO BE FILLED WITH STRONG REVELATION THAT WILL LEAVE THE READER NOT ONLY ENLIGHTENED BUT ABLE TO EMBRACE HIS WORDS AND RUN WITH THEM.
KEEP YOUR HANDS TO THE PLOW APOSTOLIC SOLDIER OF THE KINGDOM!

Apostle Ivory Hopkins

aka

"The General of Deliverance"

Overseer & Founder of Pilgrims Ministry of Deliverance

Georgetown, Delaware

INTRODUCTION

We are made in His image and created after His likeness, called to multiply, replenish, subdue and have dominion. {Gen. 1:26-28} In light of these decrees upon our lives as believers, these questions should be asked. Have we brought to life these words, causing them to take there place amongst our regions ? Have we manifested these blessings of the Lord sharing them throughout the land and its people ? Are we only working out OUR own souls salvation and leaving the rest of Zion to fend for themselves? Have we been erecting Babylonian structures {buildings} instead of enlarging God's kingdom. {Gen. 1:26-28; 11:4-5; Ez. 8:36; 1 Cor. 3: 10-17; Phil. 2:12 }

If we have truly been overtaken and are governed by the commission of the Lord Jesus Christ then why are our neighborhoods, communities, cities, etc. in a continued state of disarray. Why are we crying peace, prosperity and healing when there is really no tangible fruit in most of our regions existing. {Gen. 1:26-28; Jer. 8:11; Mat. 10:1-8; 28:19-20; Mk. 16:15-18; Jn.: 15:16}

It is the Father's good pleasure to give us the kingdom, and truly He has done just that, for His kingdom lies within us. It is we who must take the very kingdom that dwells within and distribute it throughout our cities. Far too long has the enemy possessed the lands of our God and His people. It is time for the remnant of worshipping warriors to stand and be accounted for. We must gather our warring weapons and sound the alarm as we march into battle. {Lk. 17:21; 12:32}

Our regions have been taken from us and our people have been used as slaves {P. O.W. s} to further the cause of the devil We must take back spiritually what naturally belongs to us. In doing so we will restore our regions back to the Lord and their natural design. God not only desires a people, but He also longs to fill all with His glory. {Ex. 1:12; Num. 14;21; Ps. 115:16; Dan. 7:18:22; 2 Tim 2:26}

God's Speed

Apostle D.L. Gaskins

TABLE OF CONTENTS

THE MISSION
I. Understanding the Mission
II. Regional Questions
III. Regional Grids & Maps

ESTABLISHING COMMUNICATION
* 5G NETWORK

I. Ministry Gifts
II. Body Gifts
III. Serving Gifts
IV. Church Offices
V. Gifts & Office Correspondence
VI. Spiritual Gift Chart
VII. Putting Gifts to work

THE CALL, CHARGE & COMMISSION
I   The Call
II The Charge
III. The Commission

GATHERING TEAMS
I. Effective Teamwork
II. Types of Teams
III. Team Weapons

MAPPING THE REGION
I. Scouting the Region.
II. Regional Surveying.
III. Regional DNA
IV. Counting the Costs.
V. Region Restriction

ENTERING THE REGION
I. Learning the language
II. Establishing travel and escape routes
III. Coming and going unannounced
IV. Set up safe houses
V. Field Units & Headquarters

A CONQUERED REGION
I. Establishing the Region
II. Harvesting the Region
III. Protecting the Region

BENCHMARKS

I. UNDERSTANDING THE MISSION
II. REGIONAL QUESTIONS
III. REGIONAL GRIDS

PROPHETIC EXHORTATION
{1 Jn., 4:4; Mat. 16:18; Rev. 12:12}

The mission a head is a challenging one, and although the enemies ahead are aware, skilled and prepared for the coming invasion they are no match for the force within you. No gate of hell will be able to stand against the armies of God. Our foe knows and understands that he has but a short time to inhabit the earth, for the light of our amour and the sound of the host of chariots are swiftly approaching. Take heart, be very bold and courageous for the hour has come for God's people to advance on to the mission fields.

UNDERSTANDING THE MISSION

⇒ What is a Mission

A ministry commissioned by a religious organization to propagate its faith or carry on humanitarian work; assignment to or work in a field of missionary enterprise; organized missionary work; a course of sermons and services given to convert the un-churched or quicken Christian faith; a body of persons sent to perform a service or carry on an activity; a group sent to a foreign country to conduct diplomatic or political negotiations; a team of specialists or cultural leaders sent to a foreign country; a specific task with which a person or a group is charged.

⇒ The Mission Requirements

{Read: Daniel 7:14, 18, 22, 27}

1. We are required to be servants of the one who has dominion, Jesus Christ. v. 14
2. We are required proclaim and reestablish the dominion of Jesus Christ. v. 14
3. We are required to take and possess the kingdom given to us through Christ. v. 18, 22
4. We are required to preserve and protect, the kingdom. v. 27
5. We are required to proclaim and walk in the dominion authority that has been given to us. v. 27 {Read: Gen. 1:28}
6. We are required to take back spiritually, what naturally belongs to us through Christ. v. 14, 18, 22, 27

{Read: Habakkuk 2:1-3}

1. We are required to possess willingness, endurance, discernment, a hearing ear and the ability to receive correction. v. 1-2
2. We are required to must possess and exercise calculation and perception. v. 1-2
3. We are required to must have communication skills, verbal and or written. v. 2
4. We are required to be *transporters* and or *transmitters* of the mission. v. 2
5. We are required to possess and exercise patience, longsuffering, belief and faith. v. 3

{Read: Matthew 5:5-10}

1. We must be able to receive and fulfill orders. v. 5-10

{Read: Luke 4:18-19}

1. We must be anointed. v. 18
2. We must carry the Spirit of God. v. 18
3. We must preach the gospel. v. 18
4. We must be sent. v. 18
5. We must heal. v. 18
6. We must preach deliverance and the recovering of sight. v. 18
7. We must set people at liberty. v. 18
8. We must preach the acceptable year of the Lord. v. 19
9. We must posses a burden for the poor, broken hearted, captive, blind, and bruised. v. 18

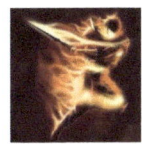

REGIONAL QUESTIONS

⇒ What is a Region?

Region: A large and indefinite part of the earths surface, a division or part, as of an organism. **A tract land;** country; **territory; portion of the body**.

{Read: Deut. 3:4; 1 Ki. 4:11; Mat. 3:5}

Each region we are assigned to carries a different assignment that will aid and or resist the campaigns against it, therefore we must be aware of their tactics. In reading *Deuteronomy 3:4* the kingdom of Og in Bashan, which were in the *region* of **Argob**, was a large kingdom and could not be underestimated. With skill and wisdom the children of Israel overtook EVERY city, which were 60 in number (threescore-20x3). The Hebrew word for *region* in this scripture is **chebel {kheh'-bel} or chebel {khay'-bel}** which means *sorrows, cord line, ropes, lot, portion, region, company, pangs, bands, destructions, pain, snare, tacklings*. This shows how some of regions were portioned off, divided into sections (cord line, ropes), to make it easy to be taken little by little. Some sections of the region they gained more equipment (tacklings) for the battle while other portions of the region may have brought *sorrow, destruction and pain*. Others were *snares* unto them. In 1 Kings 4:11, the *region* of **Dor**, region meaning **naphah {naw-faw'}** *a lofty place, height, sieve, winnowing* implement used the instruments of *pride* (lofty place, height), *division* (sieve, winnowing) to thwart the campaigns against it.

Lastly, bare this in mind as well. **Some regions were designed to come to us as we remain stationary that we may be become prophetic ports for those who need to be serviced**. {Read: Mat. 3:5} We must be careful not to go into places we are not sent to that time is not wasted or cause unnecessary warfare and loss. {Read: Acts 16:6-7} * See *Mapping the Region*, section 3 Regional DNA

⇒ <u>Where are we sent</u>

{Read: Matthew 28:19}

1. We are sent to regions, cities, nations, the world. v. 19 {Read: Mat. 3:1; 10: 5-6; Mk. 16:15}

⇒ <u>Who are we sent to</u>

{Read: Exodus 3:10}

1. We are sent to the Pharaohs {strongmen} of each region. v. 10 {Read: Mat. 12:29}

{Read: Jeremiah 1:10, 18}

1. We are sent to **people**, {all the persons of a racial or ethnic group, nation, race, certain place, group, class, ones family or relatives; human beings} **nations** {a stable community of people with a territory, culture and language in common; people united under a single government; country} and **kingdoms** {countries headed by a king or queen; monarchy, realms or domains; any of the three divisions all natural objects have been classified for example, **animal** *kingdom*, **vegetable** *kingdom*, **mineral** *kingdom*. v. 10 {Read: Luke 5:1-6}

2. We are *sent to* the whole of creation, to every creature and or life form in it. {Read: Mk. 16:15; Col. 1:15-23}
3. We are sent to sent to this world and to the worlds beyond. {Read: Acts 17:6; Rom. 8:19; 1 Cor. 15:40; 2 Cor. 5:17; Gal. 6:15; Heb. 1:2; 11:3}
4. We are sent to the *political, religious* and *social* arenas of each region. v. 18

{Read: Ezekiel 2:3-5, 7}

1. We are sent to God's elect and chosen children. v. 3 {Read: Jud. 6:14}
2. We are sent to Rebellious nations. v. 3, 5
3. We are sent to Transgressors. v. 3
4. We are sent to Impudent and stiff hearted people. v. 4
5. We are sent to people who can't and don't want to hear what we have to say. {deaf/dumb}. v. 5, 7

{Read: Luke 4:18}

1. We are sent to the poor, broken hearted, captive, blind, and bruised, {naturally or spiritually speaking}. v. 18

⇒ What are we sent to say and or do?

{Read: Ezekiel 2:4}

1. We are only to say and do what God says and or does. v. 4 {Read: Rom. 15:18}

{Read: Ezekiel 34:1-2}

1. We are to release to others what we have received from God. v. 1
2. We are to prophesy to the leaders and the people. v. 2
3. We are sent to speak messages that will not always be good. v. 2 * *Pretty prophecies*

{Read: Jeremiah 1:10; 31:28}

1. We are sent to root out, pull down, destroy, throw down, build and plant. v. 10 {Read: Jeremiah 31:28}

{Read: Matthew 10:7-13; 28:19-20}

1. We are sent to raise the dead, cleanse the lepers {diseased}, cast out devils and freely give. v. 7-8 {Read: Mk. 16:17; Lk. 13;32}
2. We are sent to trust and depended on the provision of the Lord. v. 9-10
3. We are sent to release peace to others. v. 11-12
4. We are sent to teach and baptize. v. 19-20 {Read: Acts 20:20; 2:38; Jn. 3:23; 4:1-2}

{Read: Mark 1:14-15; 16:17-18}

1. We are sent to preach the gospel of the Kingdom of Heaven and God.
2. We are sent to preach the gospel of repentance. v. 14-15 {Read: Mat. 3:2; 10:7}
3. We are to speak with new tongues and lay hands on the sick. {Mk. 16:17-18}

{Read: Luke 4:18-19}

1. We are sent to preach, heal, recover, and set people free. v. 18-19

{Read: Galatians 1:17}

1. We are sent to reveal Jesus Christ. v. 17
2. We are sent to preach Christ to the sinner. v. 16
3. We are NOT sent to confer with man. v. 16-17

⇒ When to go & When to leave.

{Read: Matthew 10:1-16}

1. We go after we have been called and empowered. v. 1
2. We go after we have receive your instructions. v.5-16 {*Read entire 10th chapter}
3. We go after we have been sent. v. 16 {Read: Mat. 11:1-2}

{Read: Acts 1:8}

1. We go after we have receive the Holy Ghost. v. 8 {Read: Jn. 20:22-23}
2. We go after we have been anointed, with God's spirit and power. {Read: Joel 2:28-29; Is. 61:1-4; Jn. 20:21-22; Acts 1:4, 8; 10:38; Lk. 4:18}

{Read: Romans 15:23}

1. It is time to leave when there is no more place in that region {area} to work {preach Christ}. v. 23 {Read: Amos 7:10}
2. It is time to leave when your assignment is over. v. 23 {Read: 2 Kin. 9:1-10; Mat. 10:14; 11:14; Lk. 24:49-51; Jn. 19:30}

In closing, there will be certain **regions** we will be told not to enter and or to be left alone. As much as we would love to minister the love of Christ to everyone everywhere, we must stick to our assignments. Some **regions** are meant to fulfill divine purpose in the lives of someone else, therefore be sensitive and sober to the Holy Spirit's direction. {Read: Deut. 2:9; Mat. 10:5-6; Acts 16:6-7} The following page I have supplied you with 4 regional maps to assist you in **intercessory prayer** and **spiritual warfare**. Understanding your regional placement is of utmost importance. Find your regional location and begin to do battle for city and state along with its regional group. Amazing things happen when prayer is instituted into our regions

REGIONAL GRIDS 1 & 2

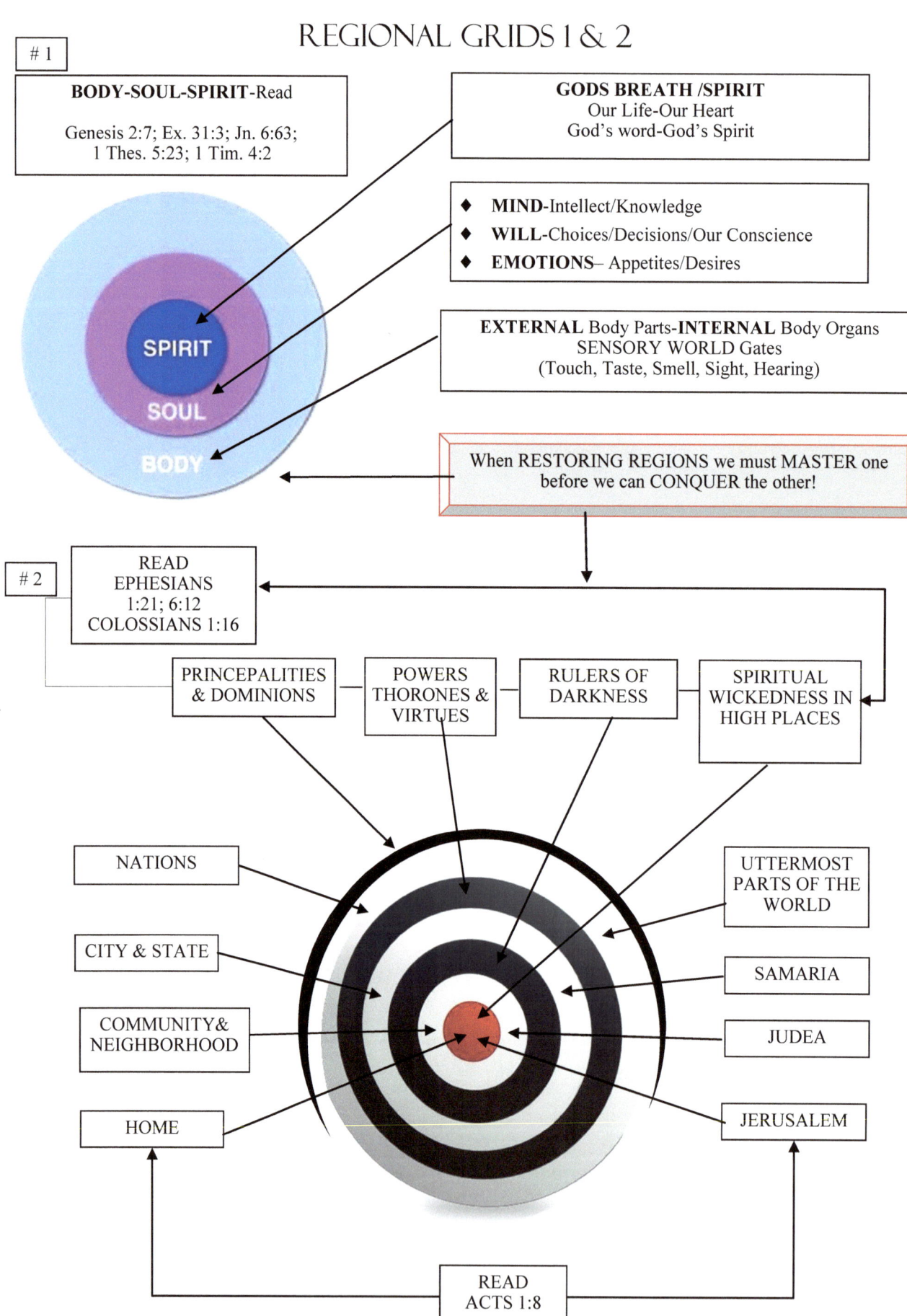

3 UNITED STATES REGIONAL MAP

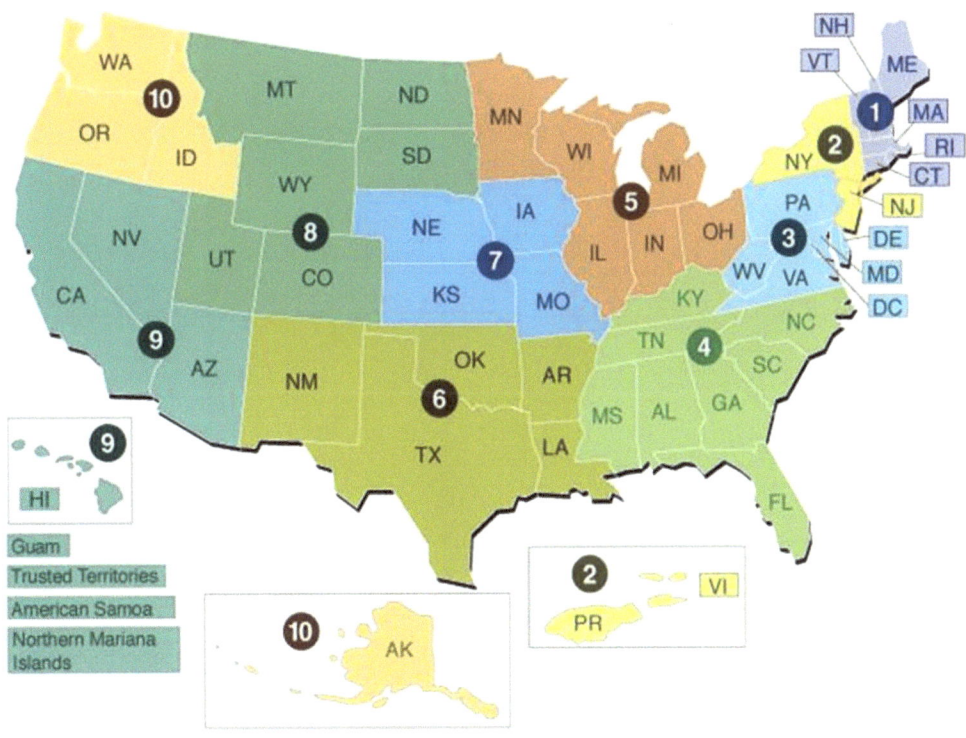

4 REGIONAL FEMA CAMPS

RESTORING REGIONS NOTES
CHAPTER 1

Take the time to write down a **power principal** or **teaching** from this chapter of the manual that sticks out to you the most.

ESTABLISHING COMMUNICATION LINES

BENCHMARKS

I. MINISTRY GIFTS
II. BODY GIFTS
III. SERVING GIFTS
IV. CHURCH OFFICES
V. GIFTS/OFFICE CORRESPONDENCE
VI. SPIRITUAL GIFT CHART
VII. PUTTING GIFTS TO WORK

PROPHETIC EXHORTATION
{Ps. 68:18; Eph. 4:11}

*Before the start of any great mission, a strong communication line must be established. Without proper communication flowing to and from the released teams greater damage will occur. I have set in the midst of you the communication lines of the Apostle, Prophet, Evangelist, Pastor and Teacher. These **gifts** I give to you are your way to have access to me. They will govern, guide, gather, guard and ground your encampments and cause them to be properly equipped. Utilize them correctly and My voice of strategy, instruction, advancement and restoration will go throughout your regions.*

MINISTRY GIFTS
{God working **BY** people}
Eph. 4:11

God has blessed the people of the earth with **gifts** and **offices**. Knowing that these conduits of God's voice exists we must note the distinct difference between the two to ensure the proper usage of them. The first part of this section of the manual we will deal with the **Gifts**. One does not have to be *saved* or *delivered* to receive *gifts* or to be placed in an *office*. The Five-Fold ministry gifts of Eph. 4:8-15 can be viewed in two spectrums, as *gifts* and or *offices*. For example; when viewed as gifts they are **5 GIFTS given to men for the body of Christ**. When viewed as offices they are **5 GIFTED MEN given to the body of Christ**. I like to call them the 5G Network. (Ps. 68:18; Rom. 11:29; Ja. 1:17)

Apostle- {Govern} Persons sent to accomplish a mission, especially the twelve apostles Jesus commissioned to follow Him. An apostle represents the one sending and has authority to represent the sender in business, political, spiritual or educational situations. {Matthew. 10: 1-2; Acts 14:14; Romans 16:7; 1 Corinthians. 4:6, 9; 12:28; 2 Corinthians 12:12; Ephesians 2:19-22; 4:11-14}

Prophet- {Guides} Reception and declaration of a word from the Lord through a direct prompting of the Holy Spirit and the human instrument thereof. Old Testament Three key terms are used of the prophet. *Ro'eh* (raah) and *hozeh* (chozeh) are translated as "seer." Raah means "to see" (as with eye) Chozeh means "one who has a vision". The most important term, *Nabi,* is usually translated "prophet." It probably meant "one who is called to speak." {Deuteronomy 18:18-22; 34:10; Matthew 16:14; 26:6; Luke 7:26; Acts 21:9-11; Ephesians 4:11-14; 1 Cor. 14} * *Prophetess* Female prophet; women serving as God's spokesperson. Five women are explicitly identified as **prophetesses**: *Anna* {Luke 2:36}, *The wife of a prophet* {Isaiah 8:3}. *Miriam* {Exodus 15:20}; *Deborah* {Judges 4:4}; *Huldah* {2 Kings 22:14}; *Noadiah*, a "false" prophetess {Nehemiah 6:14}; and *Jezebel* claimed to be a prophetess {Revelation 2:20}. Prophets and prophetess are SEERS, VISIONARIES or SPEAKERS that have been given the power and authority to access the lives of individuals through HINDSIGHT (past) INSIGHT (present) FORSIGHT (future) so that revealing the intent of the heart can manifest, worship & glory to the Father and validation to the prophet. {1 Cor. 14:25-26} *Words of wisdom* (from past) *Words of knowledge* (in present) *Words of forth telling* (for future) are all part of the function of the prophetic.

Evangelist- {Gathers} Preacher of the gospel, one who proclaims good news. The special ability to proclaim the gospel of salvation so effectively that people not only hear but respond to Christ in conversion and discipleship {Isaiah 61:1-3; Matthew 4:17; Acts 8:5-6; 14:21; Ephesians 4:11-14; 2 Timothy 4:5} There are two phases of evangelism; 1. *Church evangelism*: **Stephen** evangelized the religious arena {church}. {Acts 6:5-15} and 2. *Secular evangelism*: **Philip** evangelized the secular arena {worldly}. {Acts 8:5-13} Both spectrums of evangelism must have a horizontal and vertical impact in the spiritual realm as well as the earth realm to see tangible fruit {souls} for God. Stephen evangelized {Acts 6:5-15; 7:1-60} Philip was an EVANGELIST. {Acts 21:8}

Pastor- {Guards} Shepherd, one who tends sheep. A keeper of sheep. The first keeper of sheep in the Bible was Adam's son Abel {Genesis 4:2}. Shepherding was the chief occupation of the Israelites in the early days of the patriarchs: Abraham {Genesis 12:16); * *Shepherdess:* Rachel {Genesis 29:9}; Jacob {Genesis 30:31-40}; Moses {Exodus 3:1}. {Ephesians 4:11; I Pet. 2:25; Heb. 13:20} The Bible mentions shepherds and shepherding over 200 times. However, the *Hebrew* word for shepherding is often translated, "feeding." Shepherds led sheep to pasture and water {Psalms 23:1} and protected them from wild animals {1 Samuel 17:34-35}. Shepherds guarded their flocks at night whether in the open {Luke 2:8} or in sheepfolds {Zephaniah 2:6} where they counted the sheep as they entered {Jeremiah 33:13}. They took care of the sheep and even carried weak lambs in their arms {Isaiah 40:11}.

Teacher- {Grounds} One who *instructs*, imparts knowledge. Teaching or exhortation on aspects of Christian life and thought directed to persons who have already made a faith commitment. Instruction {*didache*} is frequently distinguished from missionary preaching {*kerygma*}. Matthew's Gospel says of Jesus, "He taught them as one having authority" {Matthew 7:29}. The Sermon on the Mount {Matthew 5-7} in particular is the rock-solid foundational teaching for Christian life {Matthew 7:24-27}. Jesus Himself admonished His disciples to make disciples, baptizing them in the name of the Father, the Son, and the Holy Spirit, "teaching them to observe all things whatsoever I have commanded" {Matthew 28:20}. Teachers carry miracles within them. {John 3:2} The special ability God gives to some to proclaim the Word of God with clarity and fearlessly. The teaching ministry is one used for the strengthening, encouragement, comfort and complete conversion of believers and unbelievers alike. {Deuteronomy 18:18-22; Luke 7:26; Acts 21:9-11; Ephesians 4:11-14; 1 Corinthians 14}

BODY GIFTS

1 Corinthians 12:7-11

Discerning of Spirits- One of the gifts of the Spirit {1 Corinthians 12:10}. It apparently refers to the God-given ability to tell whether a prophetic speech came from God's Spirit or from another source opposed to God. {Discernment} The special ability to know with assurance whether certain behavior said to be of God is divinely inspired, human or satanic. {Matthew 16:21-23; Acts 5:1-11; 16:16-18; I Corinthians 12:10; I John 4:1-6} Discerning of spirits is having the ability to discern human, demonic, and heavenly spirits that are in operation.

Faith- The ability God gives to some to know what he wants done and to sustain an unwavering confidence that God will do it regardless of obstacles, challenges or circumstances. {Acts 27:21-25; I Corinthians 12:9; Romans 4:18-21; Hebrews 11}

Gifts of Healing- The ability God gives to someone to cure illness, and restore health apart {separate} from the use of natural means. {Matthew 10:5-10; Mark 6:7-13; Luke 9:1-6; Luke 13:32; Acts 2:1-13; Acts 19:1-7; 1 Corinthians 12:10; 14:13, 19} Two types of healings: *divine intervention* {hand of doctors} and *divine healing* {hand of God} when divine intervention fails divine healing steps up. Man's extremity becomes God's opportunity. {Luke 8:43-48}

Gift of Miracles- The God given ability to serve as a human intermediary through whom He please to perform acts of super-natural power that are recognized by others have altered the ordinary course of nature and authenticated the divine commission. {Acts 9:36-42; 20:9-12; I Corinthians 12:9; Hebrews 2:4}

Gift of Prophecy- The God given ability to proclaim the Word of God with clarity and to apply it fearlessly with a view to the strengthening, encouragement and comfort of believers and the convincing of unbelievers. {Deuteronomy 18:18-22; 34:10; Matthew 16:14; 26:6; Luke 7:26; Acts 21:9-11; Ephesians 4:11-14; 1 Cor. 14}

Helps- In addition to the usual sense of assistance, the KJV used helps in two technical senses: for equipment used to secure a ship in storm (Acts 27:17) and for a gift of ministry (1 Corinthians 12:28). Modern translations understand the "helps" of Acts 27:1 in various senses: ropes (NIV, TEV); supporting cables (NAS); tackle (REB); or generally as measures to under gird the ship (NRSV). The helps of 1 Corinthians refers to the ability to offer help or assistance. In the Septuagint, God is known as the help of those who lack strength and live in poverty. It has been suggested that Paul refers to the ministry of the deacons who care for the poor and the sick. A general reference to all those who demonstrate love in their dealings with others is possible.

Interpretation of Tongues- The God given ability to make known the message of one who speaks in tongues. {Acts 2:4-11; 19:1-7; 21:37-40}

Tongues- The God given ability to speak in a language they have never heard, learned {be taught} in prayer, praise and/or communication, which translates a message from God to His people. {Acts 2:1-13; Acts 14:6-12; 19:1-7; 21:37-40 1 Corinthians 12:10; 13:1; 14:13, 19} Types of tongues: *Diverse Tongues:* {1 Cor. 12:10} *New Tongues:* {Mark 16:17} *Other Tongues:* {Acts 2:4; 21:37-40} *Unknown Tongues:* {I Corinthians 14:13} *Tongues of men and Angels*: {1 Corinthians 13:1}; *Stammering tongues* {lips} {Is. 28:11; 32:4; 33:19) *Cloven tongues*: (Acts. 2:3) *Tongue of the Learned* (Is. 50:4) *Tongues of fire* {Jer. 5:14; Ja. 3:5) Jesus Christ also spoke in tongues. {Matthew 27:46} *Eli, Eli, Lami, Sabathani* meaning: "My God, My God why has thou forsaken me". Eli, Eli, lama sabachthani. **The Hebrew form**, as Elio, Elio, etc., is the Syro-Chaldaic (the common language in use by the Jews in the time of Christ) of the first words of the twenty second Psalm; they mean "My God, My God, why hast thou forsaken me?" of Hebrew origin, {Mark 5:41} *Talitha Cumi* meaning: "damsel {o maiden, young girl} arises". Transliteration of **Aramaic phrase**. The Aramaic reflects Mark's attempt to preserve the actual words of Jesus, who probably spoke Aramaic rather than Greek in which most of the New Testament is written.{Mark 7:34} *Ephphatha* meaning: "be opened". Transliteration of **Aramaic phrase. Tongues can cast out devils**!

Word of Knowledge- The God given ability to give some one a words to discover, analyze and clarify truth and ideas, which are relevant to the growth and well being of believers. Translation of several Hebrew and Greek words covering a wide range of meanings: intellectual understanding, personal experience, emotion, and personal relationship {including sexual intercourse, Genesis 4:1, etc.}. Knowledge is attributed both to God and to human beings. {Acts 5:1-11; I Corinthians 2:14; 12:8; II Corinthians 11:6; Colossians 2:2-3}

Word of Wisdom- The God given ability to give some to know the mind of the Holy Spirit in such a way as to receive insight into how given knowledge may best be applied to applied to specific needs in the Body of Christ. {Acts 6:3-10; I Corinthians 2:1-13; 12:8; James 1:5; II Peter 3:15}

SERVING GIFTS
{God working IN people}

Motivational Gifts
Romans 12:4-8

Administration- A spiritual gift God gives to some members to build up the church 1 Corinthians 12:28 NAS, NIV, RSV), called "governments" in KJV. The Greek word *kubernesis* occurs only here in the Greek New Testament. It describes the ability to lead or hold a position of leadership. 2. NAS translates Hebrew idiom "to do justice" as "administer justice" {2 Samuel 8:15; 1 Kings 3:28; 1 Chronicles 18:14}. Similarly, NAS translates *the idiom* "to judge justice" as "administer justice" {Jeremiah 21:12}. NIV goes further with other Hebrew and Aramaic idioms translated as "administer." The person called in Hebrew "who is over the house" NIV calls the "palace administrator" {2 Kings 10:5}. The Old Testament seeks to lead people in authority to establish a society in which God's law brings fairness and justice to all people without favoritism and prejudice. 3. KJV speaks of differences of administrations {1 Corinthians 12:5}, translating the Greek, *diakoion*, "services" {NIV, RSV} or "ministries" {NAS}. Leading a church involves ministering to or serving the needs of its members.

Artistry- the gift that gives the believer the skill of creating artistic expressions that produce a spiritual response of strength and inspiration. {Exodus 31:1-11, Psalm 149:3a}.

Celibacy- Abstention by vow from marriage. The practice of abstaining from marriage may be alluded to twice in the New Testament. Jesus said that some have made themselves eunuchs for the sake of the kingdom and that those who were able to do likewise should do so {Matthew 19:12}. This statement has traditionally been understood as a reference to celibacy (See Eunuch). Paul counseled the single to remain so {1 Corinthians 7:8}. Both Jesus {Mark 10:2-12} and Paul {1 Corinthians 7:9,1 Corinthians 7:28,1 Corinthians 7:36-39; 1 Corinthians 9:5}, however, affirmed the goodness of the married state. One New Testament passage goes so far as to characterize the prohibition of marriage as demonic {1 Timothy 4:1-3}.

Dance: rhythmic movement often performed to music, dancing enjoyed a prominent place in the life and worship of Israel. Various Hebrew words in the Old Testament used to express the idea of dance seem to imply different types of movement: to skip about (*raqadh*, Job 21:11), whirling about (*karar*, 2Samuel 6:14, 2 Samuel 6:16), and perhaps twisting or writhing (*makhol*, Psalm 30:11). Pictured in the homecoming welcome of victorious soldiers by women, dancing could be accompanied by song and instrument music (1 Samuel 18:6). Exodus 15:20 celebrates Israel's deliverance at the Sea of Reeds by dancing with singing and musical accompaniment. Judges 21:16-24 accords dancing a role in the celebration of the yearly feast at Shiloh, and David is pictured as dancing before the Lord as the Ark was brought to Jerusalem (2 Samuel 6:14). Psalm 150:4 calls God's people to praise Him with the dance. As in Israel, dancing was a part of the religious practices of other peoples in the ancient Near East. Male and female dancers are known to us from Egyptian reliefs, and cultic dancers are attested in Mesopotamian texts. As an idolatrous act, dancing is mentioned in the golden-calf story (Exodus 32:19) and in the worship of Baal at Carmel (1 Kings 18:26). In the New Testament, the return of the prodigal son was celebrated with music and dancing (Luke 15:25). The practice of dancers entertaining at royal courts in Hellenistic and Roman times is attested by the dance of Herodias' daughter, Salome, (Matthew 14:6). **Mahol** (may' hahl) Personal name meaning, "place of Dancing." The name belongs to the father of three renowned wise men (1 Kings 4:31). An alternate interpretation takes the phrase "sons of the place of dancing" as a title for those who danced as part of the Temple ritual (compare Psalm 149:3 ; Psalm 150:4). The wisdom of the Temple dancers may be akin to the prophetic wisdom associated with musicians (1 Samuel 10:5; 2 Kings 3:15; and especially 1 Chronicles 25:3).

Encouragement- to fill with courage or strength of purpose especially in preparation for a hard task. {Read: Deut. 3:28}

Exhortation- Argument {Acts 2:40} or advice intended to incite hearers to action. The ability to exhort or encourage to action is a spiritual gift {Romans 12:8 {sometimes associated with prophets/preachers {Acts 15:32; 1 Corinthians 14:3}. Mutual exhortation is the responsibility of all Christians {Romans 1:12; 1 Thessalonians 5:11; 1 Thessalonians 5:14; Hebrews 3:13, Hebrews 10:24-25}. The Hebrew Scriptures provided New Testament preachers with a source of exhortation {Romans 15:14; Hebrews 12:5-6}. The synagogue sermon was described as a "word of exhortation" {Acts 13:15}. As such it called for applying the truths of the scriptural text to life. Indeed, exhortation is the goal of orderly worship {1 Corinthians 14:31}. Letters of exhortation were common in the ancient world. Messengers often supplied additional encouragement to supplement the written message {2 Samuel 11:25; Ephesians 6:22; Colossians 4:8}. Two New Testament documents describe themselves as exhortations {1 Peter 5:12; Hebrews 13:22}. The effect of the letter of the Apostolic Council was similarly described as exhortation (Acts 15:21). Though it does not designate itself as such, the Epistle of James is an exhortation.

Flags/Banners are the declarations of the kingdom that bare them. They are marked with different insignias they are used for worship and warfare. When utilized correctly they can bring glory and worship the King and fear and intimidation to our enemies. {Read: Ps. 60:4; Sng. 2:4; Is. 13:2}

Giving- A favor or item bestowed on someone. Gifts were given on numerous occasions for a variety of purposes: as dowry for a wife (Genesis 34:12); as tribute to a military conqueror (2 Samuel 8:2); as bribes (Exodus 23:8; Proverbs 17:8; Isaiah 1:23); as rewards for faithful service and to insure future loyalty (Daniel 2:48); and as relief for the poor (Esther 9:22). Since gifts might be required by custom, law, or force, modifiers are sometimes used to specify gifts given voluntarily: "willing" or freewill offerings or gifts (Exodus 35:29); free gift or "gift by grace" (Romans 5:15-17; Romans 6:23); bountiful gift not motivated by covetousness (2 Corinthians 9:5). the use of the gift of giving is for the furtherance of Christ's kingdom (1 Timothy 4:14; 2 Timothy 1:6-11); and a life of good works (Ephesians 2:10). Both Testaments witness to God as the giver of every good gift (1 Chronicles 29:14; James 1:17).

Hospitality- To entertain or receive a stranger (sojourner) into one's home as an honored guest and to provide the guest with food, shelter, and protection. (Deuteronomy 23:16-17) **Examples of Hospitality** Abraham and the three visitors (Genesis 18:1-8), Lot and the two angels (Genesis 19:1-8), Abraham's servant at Nahor (Genesis 24:17-33), Reuel and Moses (Exodus 2:20), Manoah and the angel (Judges 13:15), Elijah and the widow of Zarephath (1 Kings 17:10-11), and Elisha and the Shunammite woman (2 Kings 4:8-11). The Pentateuch contains specific commands for the Israelites to love the strangers as themselves (Leviticus 19:33-34; Deuteronomy 10:18-19), and to look after their welfare (Deuteronomy 24:17-22). **Reasons for practicing hospitality:** was that the Israelites themselves were once strangers in the land of Egypt. It was a duty of Christians (Romans 12:13; 1 Peter 4:9). It was a natural expression of brotherly love (Hebrews 13:1-2; 1 Peter 4:8-9) and a necessary tool of evangelism. A characteristic of bishops and widows (1 Timothy 3:2; 1 Timothy 5:10; Titus 1:8) **Rewards for hospitality:** Rahab's (Joshua 6:22-25; Hebrews 11:31; James 2:25). **Punishment due to no hospitality** (Genesis 19:1-11) and Gibeah (Judges 19:10-25). The only exception was Jael who was praised for killing Sisera (Judges 4:18-24). **Hospitality backbone of Christ's ministry and His church** (Matthew 8:20; Luke 7:36; Luke 9:2-5; Luke 10:4-11). and a Furthermore, one might even entertain angels or the Lord unawares (Hebrews 13:2; Matthew 25:31-46).

Intercession- The act of intervening or mediating between differing parties; particularly the act of praying to God on behalf of another person. One of the greatest prophetic models of intercession was that of Abraham. Abraham asked God not to destroy Sodom in order to save his nephew Lot. He called on the righteous character of God, asking if God would "slay the righteous with the wicked" (Genesis 18:25).

Leadership- the office or position of a leader; capacity to lead; the act or an instance of leading. {Acts 7:10; Romans 12:8; I Corinthians 12:28; I Timothy 5:17}

Martyrdom- The special ability God gives to some one to undergo suffering for the faith even to the point of death while consistently displaying a joyous and victorious attitude which brings glory to God. {I Corinthians 13:3; Acts 7:54-60; 12:1-5}

Mercy- Compassion for the miserable. Its object is misery. By the atoning sacrifice of Christ a way is open for the exercise of mercy towards the sons of men, in harmony with the demands of truth and righteousness (Genesis 19:19; Exodus 20:6; 34:6,7; Psalms 85:10; 86:15,16). In Christ mercy and truth meet together. Mercy is also a Christian grace (Matthew 5:7; 18:33-35).

Missionary- a person undertaking a mission and especially a religious mission. The special ability God gives to some to minister whatever other spiritual gifts they may have in another culture. {Acts 13:2-3; Ephesians 3:1-7; Romans 10:15; 1 Corinthians 9:19-23}

Music-Vocal & Instrumental: {Vocal} the gift that gives a believer the capability and opportunity to present personal witness and inspiration to others through singing. {Psalm 96:1-9, Psalm 100:1-2, Psalm 149:1-2}. {Instrumental} the gift that inspires a believer to express personal faith and provide inspiration and comfort through the playing of a musical instrument. {Psalm 33:1-5, Psalm 150, I Samuel 16:14-23}.

Service- Work done for other people or for God and the worship of God. Jacob worked for Laban seven years for each of his wives (Genesis 29:15-30). Service could be slave labor (Exodus 5:11; Leviticus 25:39; 1 Kings 12:4; Isaiah 14:3 compare Lamentations 1:3), farm work (1 Chronicles 27:26), or daily labor on the job (Psalms 104:23). It could be service of earthly kingdoms (2 Chronicles 12:8; compare 1 Chronicles 26:30), of God's place of worship (Exodus 30:16; compare Numbers 4:47; 1 Chronicles 23:24), of God's ministers (Ezra 8:20), and of God (Joshua 22:27). Not only people do service; God also does service (Isaiah 28:21). Even righteousness has a service (Isaiah 32:17). Service at its best is worship. This involves the service of Temple vessels (1 Chronicles 9:28), of worship actions (2 Chronicles 35:10) compare Exodus 12:25-26), of bringing offerings (Joshua 22:27), of priestly work (Numbers 8:11). Interestingly, the Old Testament never ascribes service to other gods. The New Testament similarly speaks of forced service (Matthew 27:32), sacrificial living (Romans 12:1; Philippians 2:17 with a play on words also indicating an offering), slave labor done for Christ's sake (Ephesians 6:7; Colossians 3:22; compare Philippians 2:30), worship (Romans 9:4; Hebrews 12:28), offerings (Romans 15:31; 2 Corinthians 9:12), and personal ministry (Romans 12:7; 1 Timothy 1:12; 2 Timothy 4:11). Hebrews 1:14 talks of the ministry of angels. Being in an army is also service (2 Timothy 2:4), and those who persecute Christ's followers think they do service for God (John 16:2).

Writing- the gift that gives a believer the ability to express truth in a written form; a form that can edify, instruct and strengthen the community of believers. Biblical References: I John 2:1-6, 12-14, I Timothy 3:14-15, Jude 3.

CHRUCH OFFICES

<u>Office:</u> A position of authority, responsibility, or trust given to an individual or individuals. **Offices** are like conduits, they are given to individuals to allow the gifts of God to flow through and to the rest of the body of Christ and not overtake it. Every believer has different GIFTS and or different OFFICES. If we remove gifted people from the offices of the corporate America businesses they will shut down and will not operate. However gifted people do not need a office in order to exercise their gift. 2 Chr. 31:18; Rom. 12:3-8}

1. **BISHOP** Hebrew Meaning: none found. Greek Meaning: Episkopeo-to oversee, to beware, look diligently to take oversight. Episkopos- a superintendent, officer in charge of the church or a church bishop, overseer, inspection for relief. Episkopay- superintendence, the office of a bishop, bishoprick, visitation. (Acts 1:20)

2. **BUTLER** Cup bearer, one who fills cups, a high court official. Modern day pulpit aid. Some denominations would view the nurse and/or armor barrier as a modern day butler. {Gen. 40:13; 1 Kin. 5:10; Neh. 1:11}

3. **DEACON{ESS}-** Church officers sanctioned by apostles ordained by bishops/elders. Male/Female helper in the church. {Acts chp. 6-8; Rom. 16:1; 1 Tim. 3:8-13}

4. **ELDER** Hebrew Meaning- Gaw-Dole– older Rab- Abundance, chief, captain, lord, master, archer. Yowm- ELDER, OLDER, LIVED LONGER Zaw-kane- TO BE OLD AGED, WAX OLD, AN OLD MAN, ANCIENT, ELDER, OLD MAN/WOMEN Seeb- TO BECOME OLDER, TO GROW GRAY, TO BE GRAYHEADED. Greek Meaning- Presbuteros- An, Elder, a senior, member of the celestial council, or presbyter, elder Soom-Presbooteros- A co presbyter, also an elder. * The mature one.

6. **JUDGE**: One authorized to hear and decide cases of law, to try govern, rule, and form an opinion.{est. by Moses: Ex. 18:13-26; Deut. 17:9}

7. **LAWYER-** Those who interpret the law. An authoritative interpreter of the Mosaic law. Characterization of the lawyers is especially harsh in Luke's Gospel: they rejected God's purpose for themselves by refusing John's baptism (Luke 7:30); they burdened others without offering any relief (Luke 11:45-46); they not only refused God's offer of salvation but hindered others from accepting it (Luke 11:52); they refused to answer Jesus' question concerning the legality of Sabbath healing (Luke 14:3). Lawyer is used in the general sense of a jurist at Titus 3:13. {Mat. 22:34-40; Lk. 10:25-37; 11:45:52; Tit. 3:13 *Christian lawyer *Zenus*

8. **MIDWIFE-** Those who assist in child birth and rearing. Midwives bring comfort to birthing mothers and stressed out fathers. Midwives assist in positioning the mother properly for childbirth. Midwifes also assist in giving the child identity. {Gen. 35:17; 38:28; Ex. 1:16}

9. **OVERSEER-** Hebrew Meaning: Oversee/Overseers: Nawtsakh- to glitter, to be eminent {as a superintendent, esp. of the temple services and its music} to be permanent, excel, chief musician {singer} oversee, {r} set forward. Sho-tare- a scribe, an official superintendent or magistrate, officer, overseer, ruler. Paw-kad- to visit, {with friendly or hostile intent} oversee, muster, charge, care for, appoint, commit, deliver to keep, have oversight, set over, officer, oversight. Paw-keed- a superintendent {civil, military or religious} which had the charge, governor, office, overseer {that} was set. Greek Meaning: Episkopos- A superintendent, officer in charge of the church, or a church, bishop, overseer, or inspection for relief.

10. **PRIEST/LEVITES** Authorized minister especially one who makes sacrifices, offerings and mediates between God and man. {Deut. 26:3;1 Chr. 6:32} lee' vitess) The lowest of the three orders in Israel's priesthood. In the earliest biblical records, sacrifices were offered by the chief of a tribe, the head of a family (Genesis 12:7-8; Genesis 31:54) or possibly by a priest at a temple (Genesis 14:18). These factors point to the total dedication of the Levites to the work of the Lord rather than the earthly concerns of making a good living. The tribe of Levi included at least three separate families: Gershon, Kohath and Merari (with the families of Moses and Aaron being treated somewhat separately from the rest of the tribe of Gershon). (Numbers 1:47-54; Numbers 3:14-39).

11. **PORTERS-** Gate keeper or doorkeeper, modern ushers. {1 Chr. 9:22-26; 26: 1-19 * Designed by David} KJV term for a gate or doorkeeper. Such persons served at city gates {2 Samuel 18:26; 2 Kings 7:10}, Temple gates {1 Chron, 2 Kings 9:22,2 Kings 9:24,2 Kings 9:26}, the doors of private homes {Mark 13:34}, and even the gate of a sheepfold {John 10:3}. See Doorkeeper.

12. **PUBLICANS-** Jew involved in tax collecting, {Mat. 9:9 * Matthew and Thomas}

13. **SCRIBE-** An expert in legal matters, transcribes legal contracts, keep records, act as custodians, collectors of temple, teachers of the law. Person trained in writing skills and used to record events and decisions (Jeremiah 36:26; 1 Chronicles 24:6; Esther 3:12). During the Exile in Babylon educated scribes apparently became the experts in God's written word, copying, preserving, and teaching it. Ezra was a scribe in this sense of expert in teaching God's word (Ezra 7:6). A professional group of such scribes developed by New Testament times, most being Pharisees (Mark 2:16). They interpreted the law, taught it to disciples, and were experts in cases where people were accused of breaking the law of Moses. They led in plans to kill Jesus (Luke 19:47) and heard His stern rebuke (Matthew 23:1). See Government; Sanhedrin; Jewish Parties; Secretary. {Jer. 32:12; 36:25-26; 1 Chr. 27:32; 2 Ki. 25:19; 2 Ki. 12:10; Ezra 7:6, 10}

14. **SHEPHERD–** Hebrew word is *Poimen* {Acts 20:17, 28; 1 Pet. 5:1-2} A keeper of sheep. The first keeper of sheep in the Bible was Adam's son Abel (Genesis 4:2).Shepherding was the chief occupation of the Israelites in the early days of the patriarchs: Abraham (Genesis 12:16); Rachel (Genesis 29:9); Jacob (Genesis

15. **TREASURER-** Those who handled the financial accounting aspects of the ministry. Treasures of the scriptures. {Neh. 13:13} Zadok, Pedaiah and Hanan {Ezra 1:8} Mithredath {Is. 22:15} Shebna {Jn. 12:6; 13:29} Judas

GIFTS & CORRESPONDING OFFICE

GIFT	CORRESPONDING OFFICE
APOSTLE	**BISHOP** (Gk) Ps. 109:8 Acts 1:25-26; Rom. 11:13; 1 Tim. 3:1
PROPHET	**PRIESTHOOD** Ex. 7:1, 19:6; 28:1,3-4; 29:9; Num. 3:10; 18:7, 28; Heb. 7:5
EVANGELIST	**DEACONHOOD** Acts 6:1-5; 21:8; 1 Tim. 3:10, 13
PASTOR	**OVERSEER/ELDER/SHEPHERD** Gen. 39:45; Neh. 11:14, 22; 12:42; Acts 20:17, 28; 1 Pet. 5:1-2
TEACHER	**SCRIBE** Ez. 7:6, 10-12; Neh. 13:13; Jn. 3:2

SPIRITUAL GIFTING CHARTS

Serving Gifts	Speaking Gifts	Sign Gifts	Other Gifts
Helps	Apostle	Miracles	Missionary
Hospitality	Prophet	Healings	Celibacy
Giving	Evangelist	Tongues	Intercession
Administration	Pastor	Interpretation of Tongues	Martyrdom
Leadership	Teacher		
Mercy	Exhortation		
Faith	Word of Knowledge		
Discerning of Spirits	Word of Wisdom		
Service	Music & Arts		
Ministry Gifts	**Manifestation Gifts**	**Motivational Gifts**	**Other Gifts**
Apostles	Word of Wisdom	Prophetic	Missionary
Prophets	Word of Knowledge	Teaching	Celibacy
Evangelists	Spiritual Discernment	Serving	Intercession
Pastors	Healings	Administration	Martyrdom
Teachers	Miracles	Giving	
	Faith	Showing Mercy	
	Prophecy	Exhortation	
	Tongues	Music/Arts/Writing	
	Interpretation of Tongues	Encouragement	
		Hospitality	

CONNECTING THE LINES
PUTTING YOUR GIFTS TO WORK

Administration: Congregation Council, Finance Staff, Sunday School Superintendent, Vacation Bible School Coordinator, Business Manager.

Artistry: Banner Making, Drama Club, Dance Ministry, Puppetry, Film, Photography, Work Crafts, Handicrafts, Decorating Team Set, Props Design Team.

Discernment: Congregation Council, Long Range Planning, Team Social Ministry, Team Peer Counseling, Support Group Facilitator.

Evangelism: Prospective Member, Visitation Evangelism Team, Advertising and Marketing, New Member Sponsor, Community Visitation.

Exhortation: Mutual Ministry Team, Hospital/Home/Institution Visitation, Tele-care Ministry, Peer Counseling Small Group Leader.

Faith: Congregational President Stewardship Team, Long Range Planning Team, Teacher, Bible study leader

Giving: Capital Campaign Steering Team, Stewardship Team, Volunteer Coordination, Giving Personal Testimony.

Hospitality: Greeter/Usher New Member Sponsor In-Home Bible Study Host Visitor Welcome/Information Center Banquet Server Fellowship Hour Host/Server

Intercession: Prayer Chain Prayer Partner Prayer Families/Prayer Circles

Knowledge: Parish Resource-Library Coordinator Nominating Team Long Range Planning Team Congregation Council

Leadership: Sunday School Superintendent Committee Chairperson (all types) Fellowship Activity Coordinator, Vacation Bible School Coordinator Congregational President Speaker: Special Events.

Mercy: Home/Hospital/Institution Visitation Transportation to Worship/Bible Study Social Ministry Team Support Group Leader Tele-care Minister.

Music-Instrumental: Band Leader/Members Choir Pianist Special Event Music Substitute Organist Vacation Bible School-Music Program.

Music-Vocal: Church Choir Vocal Ensemble Sunday School Song Leader Vacation Bible School Song Leader.

Pastoring (Shepherding): In-Home Bible Study, Leader New Member Sponsor, Young-Adult Counselor, Small Group Leader, Tele-care Minister.

Service (Helps): Computer Programmer/Data Entry Newsletter Collation P.A./Sound System Technician Tape Recording Worship Services Child Care Building/Grounds Upkeep Kitchen Cleaning Team Providing Transportation.

Skilled Crafts: Building Maintenance/Upkeep Electrical/Masonry/Plumbing/Roofing Mechanical Repair/Maintenance Audio/Visual Operator and Repair Computer Maintenance, Web-Page Developer.

Teaching: Adult Bible Class Teacher Sunday School Teacher Teen Bible Class Teacher Vacation Bible School Teacher Conference/Seminar Leader.

Writing: Newsletter Article Writer Newsletter Editor Public Relations/Publicity Committee Letter Writing

Wisdom: Long Range Planning Team Congregation Council Peer Counselor Support Group Leader Mutual Ministry Team.

RESTORING REGIONS NOTES
CHAPTER 1

Take the time to write down a **power principal** or **teaching** from this chapter of the manual that sticks out to you the most.

_____
_____
_____
_____
_____
_____
_____
_____
_____
_____
_____
_____
_____
_____
_____
_____
_____
_____
_____
_____
_____
_____
_____
_____

CHAPTER 2:
The Call
The Charge
The Commission

BENCHMARKS

I. HEARING THE CALL
II. RECEIVING THE CALL
III. DOING THE CALL

PROPHETIC EXHORTATION
(Mk. 16:15-18; Lk. 9:21)

Come warriors with your warring weapons in hand, to fight against the host of hell that has infiltrated my bride and her lands. Begin at my sanctuary! Release my people from their bounds, Destroy all the works of the darkness, storm the gates of Hell, they will not stand against you my beloved and truest ecclesia. Continue to advance my kingdom and the people therein. Move forward to the next portion of land. Be bold, be vigilant, wise, and very courageous. Fear not, for My spirit that is calling you, will be with you.
For the mouth of the Lord has spoken it.

THE CALL OF GOD

⇒ What is a Call

Dictionary.com says that a call is **an act of calling with the voice**; an instrument used for calling; **a request or command to come or assemble**; **a summons** or signal on a drum, bugle, or pipe; **an invitation to become the minister of a church or to accept a professional appointment**; a divine vocation or strong inner prompting to a particular course of action; the attraction or appeal of a particular activity, condition, or place; an order specifying the number of men to be inducted into the armed services.

I am lead to believe that the Call of God is basically **the purpose of the believer** {job description} here on earth. The call of God can be broken down into the following components:

Who are you called to be?
What are called to do?
Where are you called to complete it?
Who are you called to?

Each question can be answered as we take a brief but revelatory look at an ensample we have in the bible in the person of the Prophet Jeremiah.

{Read: Jeremiah 1:5, 10, 15, 18}

{v. 5} Before I formed thee in the belly I knew thee; and before thou camest forth out of the womb **I sanctified thee, and I ordained thee a prophet unto the nations.** {v. 10} See, **I have this day set thee over the nations** and **over the kingdoms**, **to root out,** and to **pull down,** and to **destroy,** and to **throw down,** to **build,** and to **plant.** {v. 15} For, lo, I will call all the **families** of the kingdoms of the north, saith the LORD; and they shall come, and they shall set every one his throne at the entering of the gates of Jerusalem, and against all the walls thereof round about, and against all the cities of Judah. {v. 18} For, behold, I have made thee this day a defensed city, and an iron pillar, and brasen walls against the whole land, against the **kings** of Judah, against the **princes** thereof, against the **priests** thereof, and against the **people of the land**.

Jeremiah is what I call an *official prophet*, through his life we can get a glimpse of how a call develops in the life of the believer. First things first, we must not confuse **WHAT** we are called **TO DO**, with **WHO** we are called **TO BE**. Jeremiah was called to **BE a PROPHET**. This portion of the call deals with *who* and *what* God has MADE Jeremiah to be, enveloping his total makeup (*character, personality,* etc.)

Next, we will find **WHERE** Jeremiah is to complete his call, **WHO** he is to execute his task upon and **WHAT** he is called to do as a *Prophet* of God. **WHERE** is found in {v.5}…..*unto the nations* and {v.10}....and **over kingdoms**. The **where** and the **who** deal with the *people* and Jeremiah's *position*, (oversight) over them as it relates to his regional sphere of influence and authority. **WHAT** he was suppose to do as a *sent-set* prophet can also be found in {v. 10} **root out, pull down, destroy, throw down, build and plant.** Jeremiah was also called to **afflict**. To *afflict* means to distress with mental or bodily pain, to torment, {Read: Jer. 31:28}

Lastly, **WHO** is Jeremiah *called to execute his call upon*. Again we must not let **WHERE** he is called to, which were **nations** and **kingdoms** overshadow, **WHO** he is called to, which can be found in......v. 15 **families** and v.18; **kings, princes, priests** and **the people of the land**.

Now the *"people of the land"* are identified by their *class* and *state*:

The **class** of people: *Families, kings, princes,* and *priests*. These are the social, political and religious arenas that Jeremiah was called for and sent to.

Notice {v. 15} says…..

For, lo, I will call all the **families** of the kingdoms of the north, saith the LORD; and **they shall come, and they shall set every one his throne at the entering of the gates of Jerusalem**, and against all the walls thereof round about, and against all the cities of Judah.

Thrones are symbolic *of haughtiness, arrogance*, and *pride*. The prophet Ezekiel also had a specific type of people he had to deal with as well, *rebellious, impudent*, and *stiff hearted*. {Read: Ezek. 2:3-8} Placing these descriptions together reveals the **state** (mindset) of the people.

The **state** of the people: *evil, prideful, arrogant* and *haughty*.

As we gather together all these components it gives to us a clear picture of the standard call of the believer would be.

Who/what are you called to be?
Prophet

What you are called to do?
Root out, pull down, destroy, throw down, build, plant and afflict.

Where are you called to complete it?
Nations and Kingdoms

Who are you called to execute it upon?
Families, kings, princes, priests and the people of the land, which were evil, haughty, arrogant, and prideful.

The bible declares in Proverbs 18:16 that… *A man's gift shall make room for him and brings him before great men.* Therefore, our ***gifts*** **are the vehicles that place us into our position to fulfill your call**.

Jeremiah's gift, *the prophet*, would set him before great men, within the ***Social arena*** *(families)*, ***Political arena*** (kings, princes) and ***Religious*** arenas (priests), to execute his call, which was to; ***root out, pull down, throw down, build, plant*** and ***afflict***. He would complete this call within each ***nation*** or ***kingdom*** God would *send* him *to* or *set* him *over*. Using the call upon the life of the prophet Jeremiah gives each believer a clear view of his or her own calling and how to cause it to manifest and be fulfilled.

This same pattern can be viewed within the New Testament church as well. In *Psalms 68:18* Christ **ascended** to heaven to **RECEIVE the** *gifts* for man from the Father. Then in *Ephesians 4:8 says* Christ **descended** and **DISTRIBUTED the** *gifts* He received from the Father to men and women alike. It is within *v. 12* where one finds the call {purpose} of these newly gifted men and women. {Read: Ja. 1:17}

The call of the new testament Ecclesia can be viewed as such;

Who/What are you called to be?   **Apostle, Prophet, Evangelist, Pastor, Teacher.** v. 11 *gifts*

What are you called to do? *perfect the saints, work the ministry and edify the body of Christ.*

Where are you called to complete the call? *The Body of Christ* and *the world.* (Read: Mk. 16:15)

Who are you called to execute the call upon? *The Body of Christ, saved and unsaved.*

Keep in mind, just as the believer's call has a beginning it also has an ending. v.13-16 * *see section on regional questions.*

Therefore, when we as the called/gifted one, has seen the manifestation of v. 13-16, we can say as Apostle Paul..

For I am now ready to be offered, and the time of my departure is at hand. **I have fought a good fight, I have finished my course** {call, assignment, job} *I have kept the faith: Henceforth there is laid up for me a crown of righteousness, which the Lord, the righteous judge, shall give me at that day: and not to me only, but unto all them also that love his appearing.* (2 Tim. 4:6-8)

HEARING THE CALL

{Read: Judges 6:11-17}

1. Sometimes angels are used as vehicles to convey our callings. v.11 {Read: Ex. 3:2; Matt. 2:18-25}
2. Our sight plays an important part in hearing from God. v. 11
3. God recognizes our strengths and weaknesses before He calls us. v. 12, 15
   {Read: Ex. 3:11: 4:10-11; Jer. 1:7-8}
4. God calls those who are working, or at least possess a willingness to work. v. 11
5. We can be unsure of what we are hearing or what we have heard. v. 17
6. When we are unsure of what God has said we can or should ask for a sign. v. 17 {Read: v. 36-40}
1. We need the grace of God to receive a sign concerning the call of God. v. 17
2. Whenever we are given a sign in light of our calling it shows the grace of God upon our life. v. 17
3. God's help comes with His callings. v. 16 {Read: v. 12; Ex. 3:12}

{Read: I Samuel 3:1-10}

1. The spirit of humility (childlikeness) allows us to hear our call. v. 1 {Read: Jas. 4:6} * *Samuel {a child, ministering before Eli and God}*
2. God's voice (calling) penetrates through the darkest darkness in our lives. v. 3
3. We are not to young or old to hear, receive or do the call of God. v. 1 {Gen. 5:3-31; 2 Chr. 24:1; Acts 7:22,30}
4. Sometimes we run from our callings. v. 4-5 {Read: Jonah 1:3}
5. Hearing the call is not the problem, knowing who's calling is. v. 4-6 {Read: Ex. 3:13-14}
6. We must answer when God calls. v. 4
7. GOD is who calls us NOT man. v. 6
8. God places seasoned saints (mature men/women of God) in our lives to help direct us in our callings, not lord over them. v. 7 {Read:. Acts 18:24-26}
9. God will allow someone else to perceive the call that your have heard and/or received. v. 8
10. Obedience is the key to hearing the fullness of the call. v. 5, 6, 9 {Read: Heb. 13:17; 1 Pet. 5:5; *obeying* elders, Acts 4:19; 5:29 *obeying* God rather than man.}
11. When we answer God, He knows we have heard Him. v. 10
12. Hearing our call holds us accountable and makes us responsible for the call. v. 10 {Read: Heb. 3:15}
13. We can't receive unless we have a clear understanding of what and/or whom we are hearing. v. 8-10
    * *Our accountability is also predicated upon our understanding.* {Read: Jer. 1:11-12; 1 Cor. 14:14-16}

RECEIVING CALL

{Read: Jeremiah 1:4-19}

1. You receive your calling first. v. 4
2. Our callings are familiar with us {know us} through the Spirit of God. v. 5
3. Before we were born we were set apart (sanctified) to receive our calling. v. 5
4. We often cannot receive our callings because we have moved from our sanctified spots {Set places}. v.5
5. The *callings* we receive are different than the *gifts* we are given. v. 5
6. Our gifts/offices are the vehicles God uses to help us perform our calling. v. 5
7. We receive our callings for others as well as ourselves. v. 5
8. Excuses keep us from receiving the call of God and all of its worth. v. 6
9. When we receive our call, God encourages, declares, and prophesies into our spirits. v. 7-8
10. We receive our own deliverance as we receive our callings. v. 8
11. We can receive our callings through the spoken word of God or the laying on of hands. v. 9 {Read: Is. 6:6-8; Ezek. 2:8-9; Rom. 1:11; 1 Thes. 2:8; 1 Tim. 4:14}
12. God will test the clarity of our reception, for He will not let us do what we have not clearly received. v. 11-13
13. When we receive our callings they come with instructions. v. 10 {Read: Rev. 10:11}
14. We can receive more than one call. v. 10 {Read: Jonah 3:1; 1 Sam. 3:10}
15. God's callings consist of *Revelation*, (v.4-5, 11,13) *Instruction*, (7-8, 16-17) *Impartations*, (v. 9-10-18) and a *Conclusion* (v. 12, 14-16, 19) * R. I. C. {pronounced *Rick*}
16. After receiving our callings God calls us forth to receive our empowerment to do the call. {Read: Mat. 10:1; Acts 1: 8; 10:38}

{Read: Revelation 3:3}

1. We must remember what we have received. v. 3 {Read: Hab. 2:1-3; Jn. 14:26}
2. We are to hold fast (obey) what we receive. v. 3
3. Repentance allows us to keep what God has given. v. 3

{Read: Judges 6:11-24}

1. Understanding increases our ability to receive our calls. v. 11
2. Our unbelief and lack of faith blocks our reception of the call of God. v. 13
3. People who have a calling on their lives usually are filled with excuses. v. 15
4. The fruit of receiving our callings is a sacrifice to God and a peace within us. v. 18-21, 23-24
5. We must beware of fear in the midst of receiving our callings. v. 22-23

{Read: 1 Samuel 3:1-10}

1. We do not have to have a vision from God to receive our callings. v. 1
2. Even if we have no vision from the Lord we must treat the callings (words) received like they are precious. v. 1
3. We cannot receive more when we don't treat what we have already preciously. v. 1
4. We receive our call to bring forth transition, usually from the old to the new. v. 2 {Read: Gen. 26; 15-22; Mat. 9:16-17}

5. The correct place {position} and/or posture plays a part in receiving and/or hearing our callings from God. v. 3, 5-6, 9 {Read: Gen. 12:1; Acts 9:3-17}
6. Before the lamp of God goes out in a people, place, nation, etc. someone will receive a call. v.3
7. God will come in person to give us our callings. v.10

{Proverbs 8:34}

1. Access to wisdom, blessings, discernment, and patience come along with callings. v. 34

DOING THE CALL

The word of God says for us to be DOERS of the word and not hearers only so this section of the manual will deal with how the believer execute what the have *heard* and *received*.

{Read: Judges 6:12-13}

1. God is with us as we do our callings. v. 12-13 {Read: Mk.16:20}

{Read: Jonah 3:5-10}

1. Whenever there is a call in the spirit, there should be a response in the natural. v.1-3 {Read: Gen. 13:14-16; Is. 61:1
2. It takes a natural willingness and obedience to operate in your spiritual calling. v. 1-3
3. We do our callings whenever, however and wherever God instructs us to. v. 3 {Read: Mat. 10:5; Mk. 16:15; Lk. 13:32}
4. When we do what we are called to do entire nations are affected. v. 5 {Read: Acts 5:28; 8:5-7; 17:6}
5. When we do what we are called to do the region will respond to our voice. v. 9 {Read: Acts 8:5-7; 17:6} * whether a bad or good response.
6. Fruit that manifest as we do our callings are, belief, repentance, prayer and fasting. v. 5
7. Doing the call allows us to release what we have heard and received from the Lord. v. 4 {Read: Ja. 1:2-23}
8. The longer it takes to do our calling, the harder it becomes to do it. {spiritual constipation}. v. 4
9. We must do our callings whether we like them or not. v. 4 {Read: Jon. 1:1-3; 4:1-2}
10. Our doing causes others to do. v. 6 {Read: Jon. 1:14-16}
11. If we do our call correctly it will cause even the greatest cities and leaders to humble themselves. v. 6
12. Doing what we are supposed to do might stop God from doing what He purposed to do. v. 9-10 {Read: Ex. 32:11-14; Jer. 4:28; Ezk. 24:13-14}

{Read: Jeremiah 1:5,10; 10:1-3}

1. Doing the call allows others to hear and receive what we have seen and heard. v. 1
2. God reveals the state of a region and its people as we do our calls. v. 2-5
3. Doing our call should exalt God and humble man. v. 6-16
4. Doing our call reveals the creative power and ability of God. v. 10-13 {Read: Is. 61:1-3; Mk. 16:20}
5. Our gifts, talents and or offices allow us to perform our callings. {Read: Jer. 1:5,10}

BENCHMARKS

I. Receiving The Charge

A. THE CHARGE OF GOD
B. THE CHARGE OF MAN
C. THE CHARGE OF ANGELS
D. THE CHARGE TO NATIONS
E. KEEPING THE CHARGE

II. Price of The Charge

A. EXAMPLES OF SUFFERING
B. PURPOSE OF SUFFERING.
C. ASSISTANCE IN SUFFERING
D. TYPES OF SUFFERING
E. REWARDS OF SUFFERING

PROPHETIC EXHORTATION
{Jn. 4:34; 9:4; Phil. 1:6; 2 Kin. 4:24; Lk. 9:62}

*I **charge** you this day to do the work of He who has sent you. For He that has begun a good work in you shall perform it until the day of the Lord Jesus Christ. Slack not your reigns, drive forward, for anyone who take hold of this plough and looks back will not be fit for My kingdom.*

PART I
RECEIVING THE CHARGE

⇒ WHAT IS A CHARGE

A charge is an **obligation**, **requirement**; management, supervision; the ecclesiastical jurisdiction (as a parish) committed to a clergyman; a person or thing committed to the care of another; **Instruction**, **command**; instruction in points of law given by a court to a jury.

⇒ THE CHARGE OF GOD

{Read: Leviticus 8:35-36}

1. We must keep the charges of God given to us. v. 35 {Read: Jn. 14:15; 1 Jn. 5:2-3}
2. Some charges of God have a time limit. v. 35 {Read: Is. 6:11-12}
3. We must remain consecrated to maintain our charges of God. v. 35-36 {Read: 1 Sam. 1:11, 26-28}
4. God keeps His charges, so we should keep ours. v. 35 *life or death!
5. When we keep our charges it helps our children keep theirs. v. 36

{Read: Jeremiah 1:9}

1. The charge of God has an entrance & an exit, our ears and mouth. v. 9 {Read: Ezek. 3:1-3}
2. The laying on of hands can impart and activate our charge. v. 9
3. God gives our charges and we must manage them wisely. v. 9 {Read: Is. 50:4; Mat. 25:14-30; Acts 4:20}
4. God will charge us despite our inabilities. v. 9 {Read: v.7; Num. 11:10-15; Jn. 16:12; 1 Cor. 3:2}
5. God doesn't leave us clueless concerning our charges. v. 9 *Key word, Behold!
6. Understanding is needed to properly execute a charge. v. 9
7. Proper and effective execution of our charge depends on our knowledge of it and our belief in it. v. 9 {Read: Ezek. 3:8}

{Read: Jeremiah 47:6-7}

1. God has recorded the time and seasons of our charges. v. 6
2. When we are walking in our charges the enemy will want you to stop, He will even make you stop yourself. v.6
3. Our charge, like our call is the word of the Lord. v. 6 {Read: 6:17; Heb. 4:12; Rev. 1:16; 19:15}
4. Our charge will not rest until it completes its mission. v. 7 {Read: 55:11}
5. When we are appointed charges, we shouldn't rest until they come to pass. v. 7 {Read: Is. 62:5-7}
6. When we stop before our charge is complete we have not receive the full burden of the charge. v. 7
7. Our charge will speak even if we try to remain silent. v. 7
8. Our charge will be most effective where it has been sent. v. 7

{Read: Matthew 9:30}

1. Though we have a charge of God, we should not want to be seen. v. 30
2. Miracles, are governed, directed, and controlled by the charge or the charge giver. v. 30
3. Our sight must be restored in order to receive a charge. v. 30 {Read: Jer. 1:11-13
4. The charges of God are straightforward. v. 30
5. Sometimes charges aren't kept. v. 31

{Read: Matthew 12:15-16}

1. A true charge markets itself, don't allow others to promote you v. 16
2. When we charge ourselves we usually promote our selves. v. 16
3. A charge proceeds a miracle. v. 15 {Read: 9:30}

{Read: Matthew 16:15-20}

1. God charges us to keep safe all He has shared with us. v. 15-19
2. God will charge us to keep secrets. v. 20

⇒ THE CHARGE OF MAN

{Read: Jeremiah 32:13-15}

1. Men can charge other men. v. 13 {Read: 1 Ki. 2:1-4; 1 Tim. 1: 18; 6:13,17; Jude 3}
2. Charges from one man to another should be done in front of witnesses. v. 13 {Read: 2 Ki. 9:1-10; Heb. 12:1; 1 Thes. 2:11; 1 Tim. 6:17}
3. A charge of man should be sealed with a word from God. v. 14 {Read: v. 14-25}
4. All charges of men should be God inspired. v. 13
5. Charges are directive words form the Lord. v. 13-15

{Read: Jeremiah 52:25}

1. Purity is a requirement of the charge of men. v. 25 * Eunuch
2. How we handle our charges plays a part in being chosen for other assignments. v. 25
3. The charge of men can bring death. v. 25

{Read: Esther 2:10}

1. Charges are given to not share everything, especially before its time. v. 10
2. Charges will come from older saints to protect us baby saints. v. 10 {Read: v. 8-10}
3. Charges come to keep us from miss managing what has been entrusted to us. v. 10 {Read: v.8-10; Mat. 7:16}
4. The charges we receive protect our calling. v. 10 {Read: Chpt. 2}
5. We must obey the charges given to us by men. v. 10

{Read: 1 Timothy 6:13; 1 Thes. 5:23}

1. All charges are to be given in the sight of God. v. 13
2. God sees the charges we are given. v. 13
3. Men can impart charges into other men/women. v. 13

{Read: 2 Timothy 4:1}

1. When we give charges to men/women we must also give instructions to those charges. v. 1 {Read: v. 2}

{Read: Matthew 22:36-40}

1. The greatest charge we will ever receive is that of loving God with all our hearts, soul and mind and loving our neighbors as ourselves. v. 36-39
2. All charges are hinged upon all of God's laws and His holy prophets. v. 40
3. If and when we fulfill these charges all others will be fulfilled. v. 40

{Read: John 15:10-12}

1. Keeping the charge of love allows us to abide in God and He in us. v. 10
2. Jesus Christ was, is and will continue to be our ensample of keeping charges. v. 10
3. The charge of love was given to us that our joy might be full. v. 11
4. Loving one another seems to be the most difficult charge to keep. v. 12 {Read: Mat. 24:12}
5. The love charge is more than words its action. v. 10-12 {Read: Ezk. 33:30-33}

⇒ THE CHARGE OF ANGELS

{Read: Genesis 24:7, 40}

1. One of the charges angels have received is to go before us and show us the way to what we are looking for. v. 7
2. God gives the charge to angels through man. v. 7 {Read: Ps. 103:20-21; Mat. 26:53}
3. God delivers us from bondage and charges His angels to keep us in our freedom. v. 7
4. Another charge of the angel is to prosper our way. v. 40
5. We must allow our angels to keep their charge. v. 7, 40

{Read: Psalms 8:5, 91:11-12}

1. Angels are not only charged over us but also to us. v. 5 {Read: Mat. 4:6; Lk. 4:10; Heb. 2:7, 9}
2. As men we have been positioned OVER angels they are charged to serve us. v. 5   *Angels:{Heb. Elohiym -el-o-heem} *God has made us a little lower than Elohiym {God}*
3. Angels are charged to keep us in our ways. v. 11
4. Angels are charged to carry us in their hands. v. 12
5. Angels are charged to get us out of circumstances before we hurt ourselves. v. 12

{Read: Judges 2:1-4}

1. Angels are charged to bring us up, out and make us go. v. 1
2. Angels are charged to deliver us out of bondage. v. 1
3. Angels are charged to take us or bring us into our destined places. v. 1
4. Angels are charged to bring us reassurance and remind us of our covenant with God. v. 1
5. Angels are charged to remind us of our purpose. v. 2
6. Angels are charged to question and expose our disobedience. v. 2
7. Angels are charged to explain the purposes of God. v. 3
8. When angels do their charge it causes men to praise and worship God. v. 4
9. Angels are charged to talk to God's people for Him. v. 4

{Read: Matthew 4:6}

1. Angels are charged to bring us out and through situations we may come upon, not just what we get ourselves in. v. 6
2. Even though we are sons and daughters of God {set over angels}, only He {the Father} can give angels a charge. v. 4 {Read: Mat 26:53}* *We pray to the Father, the Father releases the angels, they move on His command based on His word that comes out of our mouth.* {Ps. 103:20-21}

{Read: Luke 4:10}

1. The charge of an angel is part of the Word of God. v. 10
2. Angel's charge are a part of the written Word of God. v. 10

{Read: Hebrews 1:14-2:1-3}

1. Angels are charged to minister {do service} for us. v. 14 * *Minister:* {Heb. *Diakonian*– to do service}
2. Angels cannot change the instructions given to them by God. {chp. 2 v. 2}
3. We cannot escape angels and their charges. v. 3

⇒ D. THE CHARGE OF NATIONS

{Read: Exodus 6:13}

1. We are given charges to and over nations and kingdoms. v. 13
2. We are never charged to a nation alone. v. 13 {Read: Neh. 7:1; Jos. 2:1-4; Mat. 21:1-6; Mark 6:7; Acts 19:21-22}* no one man, ministry, etc. can fulfill a charge alone.
3. When we are charged over a nation/region we are charged to the leader of that particular place. v. 13 {Read: Jon. 3:5-10; Rev. 10:11} *spiritually& naturally speaking.*
4. Our charges come with instruction. v. 13 {Read: Jer. 1:10}
5. Our charges were designed to bring a people out of the place of bondage. v. 13

{Read: Nehemiah 7:2}

1. A charge to a nation/region is given to some one who is faithful and God fearing. v. 2
2. Our charges should even effect to our own cities. v. 2 {Read: Jonah chapters 1-3; Acts 1:8}

{Read: 1 Chronicles 22:12}

1. Ask God for His understanding and wisdom concerning our charges. v. 12
2. The laws of God are kept and established as we keep our charges. v. 12
3. We should not accept national charges given by men that are not lead by the spirit. v. 12
4. God knows when we are able to handle a national charge. v. 12
5. As fathers (natural/spiritual) we should prepare and leave all things that our children need (natural/spiritual) to fulfill their charges that God has given them in life. v. 12 {Read: v. 13-19}

{Read: Jeremiah 1:10}

1. A national/regional charge deals with a systematic setting. v. 10
2. We are not only charged to nations/regions, but also to the kingdoms within and over them. v. 10
3. National charges deal with rooting out, pulling down, destruction, throwing down, building and planting, but not always in this order. v. 10 {Read: 31:28}
4. God makes sure we see, have a clear picture/understanding, where and to whom He as charged us to. v.1
5. Our charge starts the day we hear/receive the initial setting or sending. v. 10

{Read: Ezekiel 2:3-10}

1. Even though God has given us charges over/to nations we are still human and can make mistakes. v. 3
2. Some nations that we will be, or are charged to, are rebellious towards God, so they will be rebellious to us also. v.3 * *Don't take it personal*.
3. When/as we deal with national/regional charges, we usually will have to combat generational sins. v. 3
4. Nations can be *imprudent* {contentious boldness, disregard for others.}; *stiff hearted*, {stubborn} and *stiff necked* {rebellious}. v. 4 {Read: Ex. 32:9; Deut. 9:6, 13; 31:27; 2 Chr. 36:13; Jer. 17:23; Acts 7:51}
5. As we keep our charges we must say only what God has said, or is saying, whether people hear or not. v.

4-6 {Read: v. 7}

6. In order to carry out our charges we must not let fear effect us. v. 6 {Read:. Prov. 29: 25-26; Mat. 10:28; Jn. 20:19; Acts 4:13-19}
7. Doing what we are charged to do reveals our gifts and callings. v. 5
8. As God gives us charges to a particular nation He also gives us the state of that nation. v. 6
9. Carrying out our charges will cause people to speak against us, there will be some sort of resistance whether through words or actions. v. 6
10. We cannot let the looks, or the actions, of the nation/region we are charged to hinder us in our quest to further Gods kingdom. v. 6
11. We have a choice to either receive or decline the charge to a nation, but both have its rewards and consequences. v. 8
12. Some times the state of the nation/region often tries to take us over we must not conform but convert. v. 8
13. We must take only what God gives us to fulfill our charge, nothing more or nothing less. v. 8 {Read: Mat. 10:9-10; Mk. 6:7-9; Lu. 10:4
14. In receiving charges to nations the hand of God must be in the midst of the appointment. v. 9 *Sent-vs-went.
15. We can see our charges because they are written throughout the word of God. v. 10
16. Our charges are not always grand and spectacular, especially dealing with different nations and regions. v. 10

{Read: Acts 1:8}

1. There will always be an endowment of power from the Holy Spirit for each charge. v.8 {Read: Mat. 10:1; Jn. 20:21-23; Acts 10:38; 1 Cor. 4:20}
2. We are not just charged to one nation/region. v. 8
3. As each believer walks out their individual callings corporately, the end result will be that the whole earth will be impacted. v. 8

{Read: Matthew 10:5-6}

1. Before we are sent we are charged. v. 5
2. We must go to the nations/regions God instructs us to. v. 5
3. The nations God sends us to are designed to respond to our presence and our voice. v. 5
4. Our/their houses can also be a nation. v. 6
5. We have a charge to keep in every nation/region to go to the lost. v. 6

{Read: Titus 1:5-9}

1. There are reasons why we are charged to certain people, nations and regions. v. 5
2. We are to give others charges as we have been charged. v. 5
3. We are charged to the nations that are in wanting. v. 5 {Read: Acts 16:9-10}
4. Fulfilling our nation charges brings order to that particular place. v. 5
5. We have a charge to ordain elders in every city to keep that nation under the rule and power of God. v. 5
6. There should be no wanting in the nations after we have completed our charge. v. 5
7. There are requirements/qualifications that we must up hold to before there is an impartation of a charge from God through man. v. 6-9

⇒ E. KEEPING THE CHARGE

{Read: Genesis 26:5}

1. When we keep the charges given to us, it automatically brings blessings upon our seed/children. v. 5
2. Our charges must be kept along with *obeying* {carrying out the word and/or will of another especially God, to submit to authority} the voice of God, His *commandments* {rules imposed by authority} *statues* {law or decree issued by a ruler or governing body or especially by God being the superior ruler} *laws* {an orderly system of rules and regulations by which a society is governed.} in order to receive the fullness of the blessings of God. v. 5 * The promises and blessings of the Lord are conditional. {Read: 2 Chr. 7:14; Is. 1:19}

{Read: 1 Kings 2:1-9}

1. As others die we are entrusted with charges that we must keep. v. 1
2. We must keep the charge given by our fathers. v. 1
3. By keeping our charges our level of maturity will show forth. v. 3
4. In keeping the charge of God we must walk in His ways, commandments, judgments, {authoritative opinions, decisions, or sentences; justices of God} testimonies, {witnesses borne on behalf of something or someone} *Hebrew word. *Edah*: a stated assemblage, family or crowd, assembly, company, congregation, multitude, people, swarm. v. 3
5. Keeping the charge brings prosperity in all that we do and wherever we go. v. 3
6. Keeping our charge allows God's word to accomplish what it was sent out to do. v. 3 {Read: Is. 55:11; 1 Tim. 1:18}
7. We must walk in truth with all our heart and soul to ward off failure and keep our charge. v. 4
8. We must keep the charge of war on the enemy, we must not let him rest for he has come to steal, kill and destroy our peace. v. 5-6 {Read: Jn. 10:10}
9. In keeping our charge we must bless those who bless us and bless those who curse us. v. 8-9 {Read: Gen. 12:3; Mat. 5:43-48; Rom. 12:14}

{Read: Ezekiel 44:8}

1. We must keep the charge of Gods holy things. v. 8
2. The people and their charge belong to God not us. v. 8
3. We cannot keep charges with impure hearts. v. 8

{Read: Mark 7:36}

1. Sometimes no matter how hard we try to keep the charge, we sometimes fail. v. 36
2. There is a reason for God giving us charges to keep. v. 36 {Read: Mk. 9:2-10}
3. God doesn't want us to bring unnecessary opposition to ourselves that's why we must keep our charges. v. 36 {Read: Mk. 5:39-43; Jn. 7:3-10}

{Read: 1 Timothy 6:20}

1. The charges we must keep are committed to our trust. v. 20
2. No matter what opposition {vain babblings, science, etc.} comes our way we must keep what has been committed unto us. v. 20
3. *Vain* {useless, empty, conceited never ending} and *profane* {to treat something holy with irreverence} *babblings* {uttering of indistinct meaningless sound, foolish chatter and/or talking, low murmuring, childish sounds} and *science* {knowledge and/or understanding} come to hinder us from keeping our charge. v. 20
4. We can only keep the charges committed to us through the Holy Spirit. v. 20 {Read: 2 Tim. 1:14}
5. God keeps what we give to Him, so we must keep what is give to us. v. 20 {Read: 2 Tim. 1:12}

PART II
THE PRICE & REWARD OF A CHARGE

⇒ The Price of the Charge.

{Read: Philippians 1:29}

* As the called of God it is important to know that when we go forth in our charge that there will be some **suffering** that you will have to go through. v. 29 {Read: Acts 14:22}

The **PRICE** of the charge is broken down into four parts.
***Examples** of suffering. ***Purpose** of suffering. ***Assistance** in suffering. ***Types** of suffering.

⇒ Examples of Suffering

- David: {Read: 1 Sam. 19:9-11; 21:10; 22:1}
- Elijah: {Read: 1 Kings 18:17-40; 19:1-4}
- Daniel: {Read: Dan. 3:14-23; 6:16}
- Jesus: {Read: Mat. 26:45, 60-68; 27:27-40}

⇒ Purpose of Suffering

1. *To advance the kingdom of God.*

   * In the book of acts the apostles were met with much opposition because of their stand and fight to establishing the Kingdom of God on earth. {Read: Acts 4:1-4,7-12,16-17}

2. *To glorify God.*

   * Stephen laid aside how he may have felt to glorify God in his work and his sufferings. {Read: Acts 6:12-15; 7:54-56}
   * Jesus prayed that this was the hour that the Father would glorify him so that the Father would be glorified. {Read: Jn. 17:1-5; 10:17-18}
   * Jesus Christ emptied Himself {made no reputation} from all His own feelings to bring glory and honor to the Father. {Read: Phil. 2:7-8}

3. *To edify other believers.*

   * Paul's sufferings brought confidence to his fellow brethren. {Read: Phil. 1:12-14}
   * Paul was comforted in his sufferings to hear that the church of Thessalonica was standing in the faith despite there own persecutions {Read: 1 Thes. 3:5-8; 2 Thes. 1:4-5}

C. ASSISTANCE IN SUFFERING

A. *The Holy Ghost*

* Stephen, noted as one of the 1st martyrs of the faith was aided during his suffering to endure not only, verbal, but also physical abuse. {Read: Acts 6:5-8}
* The apostles were filled with the Holy Ghost to receive power to give them an ability to go through whatever came there way in advancing the Kingdom of God. {Read: Acts 1:8}

B. *Prayer*

* A solid prayer life is needed in fulfilling our charges, for prayer gives us insight and a peace within the will of God, even when we are faced with persecutions. {Read: Mat. 26:39-45}

C. *Faith*

* We must have and keep the faith in believing that our heavenly father will bring us out and keep us through our suffering. {Read: Heb. 11:1-6}
* We must keep our faith secure in the promises of God to reward us for our endurance through persecution, even repaying those who the persecution comes from. {Read: 2 Thes. 1:5-6} Our faith + work= faithfulness. {Read: Ja. 2:14-26}

D. *The Word of God*

* The Word of God is a great comforter to us, for it is these very words we can stand and take hold of, in the time of trouble and persecution. {Read: Mat. 4:4, 7, 10; Heb. 4:11}

TYPES OF SUFFERING

A. *God Ordained*

* The God ordained suffering is apart of our belief system that was designed for every believer's life. {Read: 1 Cor. 12:29; Phil. 1:29; 2 Tim. 2: 12}
* Suffering is a part of the will of God. {1 Pet. 4:19}
* God ordained suffering fulfills the scriptures {the prophetic words} written and/or spoken concerning us. {Read: Mat. 26:47-54; 27: 35; Mk. 14:46-49; Lk. 22: 47-53; Jn. 18:1-11}
* God ordained suffering produces wisdom, obedience and fellowship. {Read: Phi. 3:10; Heb. 5:8}

B. *Self inflicted*

* Not all suffering is of God. {Read: Ex. 12:23; Lev. 19:17; Ps. 105:14; 1 Cor. 10:13}
* We inflict ourselves by doing things out side the will of God. *i.e. disobedience* {Read: Deut. 28:15-66; Prov. 19:15; Rom. 6:23; Gal. 6:7; 1 Pet. 4:15-16}
* We can self inflict ourselves for the furtherance of the gospel. {Read: Mat. 17:17; 19:12; Heb. 11:25}

E. REWARD OF SUFFERING

A. *Dispensation of the Gospel*

* *Dispensation:*

    English: A period of time under which mankind is answerable to God for how they have obeyed the revelation of God which it has received. A stewardship entrusted to one.

    Greek: oikonomia-administration.

* Our rewards can be either beneficial or detrimental to our walk with God. {1 Cor. 9:17; Read: Eph.1:10; 3:2; Col.1:25}

B. *Prosperity*

English: A state of material or spiritual abundance.

Hebrew: *Towb*-Good, well; *Tsalach*-to push forward; *Shalev*-careless, carefree, security; *Shalvah* security, ease; *Shalowm*-safe, well, health, prosperity.

* God will prosper us in what ever we do and where ever we go if we keep our charges even through suffering. {1 Ki. 2:3-4}

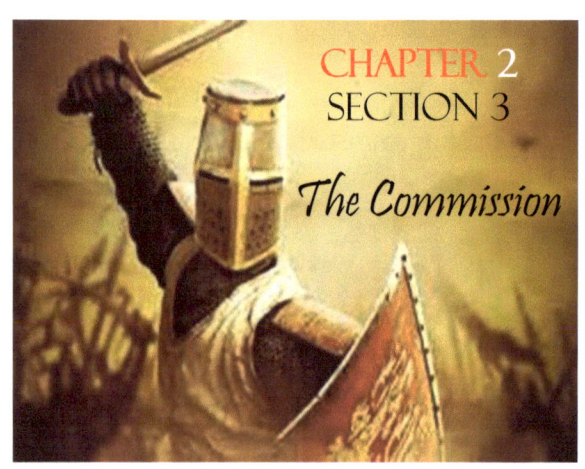

BENCHMARKS

A. REQUIREMENTS
B. GOD TO MAN
C. MAN TO LOST/CHURCH
D. CHURCH TO NATIONS
E. NATIONS TO NATIONS

PROPHETIC EXHORTATION
{Mat. 28:19-20}

Beloved, take the King's commissions and distribute them to the governors and lieutenants throughout the nations. Further My household and My people. For this is the hour that I am sending my sons and daughters forth with power and authority to deliver My lands from their present despair. {Ezra 8:36}

A. RECIREMENTS OF COMMISSION

⇒ Commission

A formal written warrant granting the power to perform various acts or duties; a certificate conferring military rank and authority; *also* **: the rank and authority so conferred;** authority to act for, in behalf of, or in place of another; a task or matter entrusted to one as an agent for another, a group of persons directed to perform some duty; a government agency having administrative, legislative, or judicial powers; a city council having legislative and executive functions; an act of committing something;

{Read: 1 Samuel 3:9-10}

{**Willing**: Done accepted or given readily without hesitation; voluntary; ready or ready to act promptly and gladly. Obedient: the carrying out of commands, to comply with a command, order or request}

1. There must be a willingness in our hearts and obedience in actions. v. 9
2. God watches our willingness and obedience towards others. v. 9
3. The fruit of respecting another's commission is to willfully obey their voice. v. 9
4. We cannot expect others to respond to our commissions if we do not respond to theirs. v. 9
5. God is moved by our willingness and obedience, it brings Him to where we are. v. 10
6. If we are not willing and obedient to voice of God through others we can miss a visitation from God. v. 10
7. Being willing and obedient pays off in the end. v. 10 {Read: Is. 1:19}

{Read: Romans 15:15-32}

{**Diligent**: Done with or characterized by great care and effort.}

1. Fulfilling our commissions diligently will make us become even bolder in reminding people why we are called, what we are called to do, where we are called, and how we are called to do it. v. 15-20
2. Care and effort towards our commissions takes us to unnamed places and people. v. 19-22
3. Hindrances will come to stop our commission, must be steadfast. v. 22
4. Diligence in our commissions shows forth through joy, expectation and desire when/before going into different cities and regions. v. 23-24
5. We must bare equal diligence fulfilling our commissions to sinner and saint. v. 26-27
6. We should not leave or come empty handed when doing our commissions. v. 28-29
7. Even those that diligently perform their commissions need prayer, for it strives with them to encourage them through the blessings and trials of their call. v. 30-32
8. All those fulfilling a commission have a desire to be delivered, accepted and refreshed no matter how diligent they may seem to be. v. 30-32

{Read: 2 Timothy 4:1-8}

{**Faithful**: Loyal, worthy of trust, accurate, truthful, *faithfulness: making faith living reality in ones life.}

1. We must be faithful to the God of our commission. v. 1
2. We must be faithful in season and out of season. v. 2
3. Our commissions doesn't change because times and seasons do. v. 2
4. We must remain faithful in **Rebuking** {a reprimand sharply for sin.}, **Reproving** {to rebuke, express disapproval of, scold, find fault with, a cutting rebuke for misconduct.} **Exhorting**, {to encourage others to commendable conduct.}

Longsuffering (bearing injuries or provocations patiently), and our **Doctrine** (teachings, principles or a body of principles, dogma) for in doing so we will produce faithfulness in others. v. 2

5. Everyone will not remain faithful to their commission. v. 3-4
6. Discernment, endurance, work and making our ministry full proof entails faithfulness to fulfill our commission. v. 5
7. We must be faithful until the end. v. 6
8. We will be rewarded a crown of righteousness for our faithfulness. v. 7-8

B. COMMISSION: GOD TO MAN

{Read: Isaiah 61:1}

1. When God gives a commission to a man He anoints them for that purpose. v. 1-3 {Read:. Mat. 10:1; Jn. 20:21-23; Acts. 10:38}
2. God has given us a commission to preach, bind, proclaim, comfort, appoint, and give. v. 1-3
3. We are to act out our commission upon the meek, poor, brokenhearted, captives, bound, blind, bruised and mourners. v.1-3
4. As Christians we carry out the same commission that was given to Jesus Christ. v. 1-3 {Read: Lk. 4:18}

{Read: John 3:16-18}

1. Love and sacrifice is what our commission is all about. v. 16
2. We must believe in God and our commission. v. 16
3. Our commission brings and gives everlasting life. v. 16
4. We are not commissioned to condemn {*to declare a person guilty and worthy of punishment; to declare unfit for use.*} the world but to save it. v. 17 {Read: Lk. 6:37}
5. We must get others to believe in our commissioner {Jesus} . v. 17
6. People are condemned because they do not believe in our commissioner. v. 18

C. COMMISSION: MAN TO THE LOST & CHURCH

{Read: Ezra 8:36}

1. We were given our commissions for a purpose, to further God's people and His House. v. 36
2. Our commissions carry within them the power of prosperity. v. 36 {* see "Reward of Suffering" for more on prosperity}

{Read: Matthew 10:5-15}

1. Our commissions entail a sending along with commands. v. 5-6
2. We can only go where we are commissioned. v. 5-6
3. Our commissions have instructions and requirements. v. 5-13
4. We must totally trust and depend on the provision of God as we fulfill our commissions. v. 8-13
5. Our commissions have a time spans. v. 14
6. Those who are commissioned will face rejection, do not take it personal. v.14
7. Those who reject the commissioned are rejecting God and setting themselves up for destruction. v. 15

{Read: Matthew 28:19-20}

1. As we believers we are commissioned to **GO**, {*proceed, move or start to move from a given place or out of someone presence; to engage in specific activity; to extend or spread; to serve.* {Read: Matt. 10:5-6; Mk. 16:15} **TEACH**, {*impart knowledge or skill to someone; instruct; cause to learn by example or experience}*. {Read: Ti. 2:12} and **BAPTISE**, {**ablution: to wash, sub-merge, dip and/or cleanse a body or part of a body in or with water.* v. 19 *Read: Mk. 16:16; Jn. 3:22-23
2. We are commissioned to the nations. v. 19 {Read: Matt. 24:14} ***Nation**: {*group of people under a sovereign government, a community of people, a tribe.*} *Hebrew.* Ummah-community, clan, tribe;
3. Authority comes along with the commission. v. 12
4. We can be commissioned by other men and women. v. 12
5. We must be lead by the Holy Spirit in commissioning men and women, for we can commission and authorize the wrong people and send them to do the wrong things. v. 12 {Read: v. 1-11}

D. COMMISSION CHURCH TO THE WORLD

{Read: Mark 16:15}

1. As the *church* at large we are commissioned to go to the world. v. 15 {Read: Jn. 17:18} *World: Our planet, also refers to that which is temporal rather than eternal. Greek: *aion*-perpetuity, ever, world; *aionois* -perpetual, long ago; *ge*- soil, region, whole earth; *kosmos*-world; *oikoumene*-roman empire.

2. Part of our commission as the *church* is proclaiming the gospel {Good News} to every creature. v.15 ***Creature*-** any created being, man included, brought into existence as a result of God's power and authority. {Read: Gen 1:3-24, Ps. 33:6; Heb. 11: 3; Jn. 1:3; 1 Cor. 8:6}

3. As we fulfill our commission by preaching {proclaiming} to the world we are taking back our rightful position of dominion that we originally received but exchanged for a lie. v. 15 {Read: Gen. 1:26-28; Rom. 1:25}

RESTORING REGIONS NOTES
CHAPTER 2

Take the time to write down a **power principal** or **teaching** from this chapter of the manual that sticks out to you the most.

Chapter 3 Gathering Apostolic Teams

PROPHETIC EXHORTATION
Jud. 20:11; Ezek. 9:1; 1 Kin. 11:24; 2:12; Acts 2:2

Gathering my people together, let them be united as one, every man with their warring weapons. Set leaders over them that they may have direction. Release them into the regions to establish My kingdom and as they enter the places I send them as a unified front, I will suddenly come and turn the places where I send them upside down.
{Is. 24:1; Acts 17:6}

BENCHMARKS

I. Effective Team work
A. TEAM PURPOSE
B. TEAM DYNAMICS
C. TEAM LEADERSHIP

II. Types of Teams
A. INTERCESSORY TEAMS
B. SCOUTING TEAMS.
C. MINSTREL TEAMS.
D. EVANGELISM TEAMS
E. DELIVERANCE TEAMS
F. SCRIBE TEAMS
G. PROPHETIC TEAMS
H. APOSTOLIC PRESBYTERIES

III. Team Weapons
A. RECEIVING WEAPONS
B. KNOWING WEAPONS
C. USING WEAPONS
D. WEAPON MAINTENANCE

I. EFFECTIVE TEAM WORK

Team: Two or more draft animals harnessed to the same vehicle or implement; *also* these with their harness and attached vehicle; a draft animal often with harness and vehicle; *obsolete* lineage, race; a group of animals; a brood especially of young pigs or ducks; a matched group of animals for exhibition; a number of persons associated together in work or activity; a group on one side (as in football or a debate); Crew Gang

⇒ A. TEAM PURPOSE.

{Read: I Chronicles 19:10-12}

1. To receive help and fresh strategies. v. 10
2. To receive help in the height of battle. v. 10
3. To allow more ground to be covered when fighting the enemy. v. 11-12
4. To enable us to surround the enemy. v. 11-12
5. To provide backup for one another. v. 12
6. Teamwork, if yield to and used correctly, destroys pride and releases humility. v. 10-12 {Read: Phil. 2-3}
7. Teamwork reveals the weak link in leadership, {exposes sin}. v. 10-12 {Read: 1 Cor. 3:1-8}

{Read: Ecclesiastes 4:8-12}

1. To establish partners, co-laborers in the earth, for the kingdom. v. 8
2. To share the wealth {fruit} of the labor. v. 8
3. To destroy the spirit of loneliness and its effects. v. 8
4. To assist in the production of the harvest. v. 8
5. To bring and ending satisfaction to our labor for the kingdom. v. 9
6. To receive our reward for laboring in the region {land} we are called in. v. 9 {Read: 1 Cor. 9:11}
7. To bear one another up in case of a fall. v. 10
8. To be the support the other needs. v. 10
9. To bring comfort, ease, security and assurance in the midst of battle. v. 11
10. To glean strength from one another. v. 11-12 {Read: Prov. 27:17}
11. To enhance our power needed to withstand the enemy. v. 12
12. To establish a covenant within leadership for the advancement of the kingdom. v. 12
13. To keep the fire, {zeal, anointing, power} burning in one another. v. 11 {Read: 2 Tim. 1:6}

{Read: Ezekiel 9:1}

1. To better effect our cities, nations, regions etc. v. 1 {Read: Acts. 17:5-6}
2. To bring the leaders of cities together. v. 1
3. To bring more weapons into the battle, better our arsenals. v. 1 {Read: Neh. 4:13-18}
4. To bring down the kingdom of darkness by destroying the works of the devil. v. 1 {Read: v. 2-7; 1 Jn. 3:8}

{Read: Amos 3:3}

1. To test the strength of your unity, for teams are as strong as its unity. v. 3
2. The purpose of a team is to bring agreement, unity and/or oneness between two or more persons. v. 3 {Read: 1 Cor. 1:10}
3. To produce a bond in the spirit that can't be easily broken by any natural circumstances or spiritual forces. v. 3 {Read: Ecc. 4:12}

{Read: 1 Corinthians 1:10}
1. To have the same speech and/or communicate the same. v. 10
2. To bring down the walls of tradition, false religion, denominationalism, etc. v. 10 {Read: 1 Cor. 3:1-9; 12:12-27}
3. To eliminate division. v. 10 {Read: 1 Cor. 3:1-3}
4. To produce a cohesiveness {unity/wholeness} in the spirit. v. 10 {Read: Jn. 71:11}
5. To walk in the same mindsets {thoughts} and judgments. v. 10 {Read: Rom. 15:5; Phil. 2:5}
6. To bring our mouths, minds and spirits into agreement. v. 10

{Read: 1 Corinthians 3:9}
1. To teach us how to be co-laborers. We can't be co-laborers with Christ if we can't be with one another. v. 9
2. To assist one another as a part of the God-team to build and advance the kingdom of God. v. 9 {Read: Ezra 8:36}

⇒ B. <u>TEAM DYNAMICS</u>

{Read: Luke 5:2-11}
1. The team members must be those that are obedient. v. 3-6
2. Team members must be good at following instructions. v. 3-6
3. Must allow Christ access to every part of their lives. v. 2-3
4. The team, nor its members, mustn't allow what they know {there intellect} to interfere with God's plan. v. 4-5
5. The team and its members must be able to hear the voice of God. v. 2-11 {Read: Mat. Chp. 10}
6. The team and its members must not be afraid to ask for help. v. 7
7. The team members are not selfish nor self centered, when one is blessed the team is blessed and when one hurts the team hurts. v. 6-7 {Read: 1 Cor. 12:26}
8. The team and it's members must possess a spirit of repentance. v. 8 {Read: Rom. 2:4; 2 Cor. 7:10}
9. The team and its members must recognize and reference {fear} the power of God. v. 8-10
10. The team and its members CANNOT be afraid of change. v. 10 {Read: Jer. 1:5; 17:16; Amos 1:1; 7:14-17}
11. The team and its members must be willing to forsake all and follow Christ. v. 11 {Read: Matt. 19:27,29}

{Read: 1 Corinthians 12:1-11}
1. No member of the team should be ignorant concerning their spiritual gifts or their teammates. v. 1
2. All team members should be planted and steadfast to avoid being lead astray. v. 2
3. Idolatry can cause members of the team to lose focus of God and His agendas. v. 2
4. Team members must be sober {alert} of the pasts of each other. v. 2
5. All team members must speak by the Spirit of God. v. 3
6. All team members must believe, confess, and possess the Lordship of Jesus Christ. v. 3
7. Each team has a diversity of gifts but all carry the same *Spirit*. v. 4
8. Each team/member will be used and managed different ways. v.5
9. The entire team is governed by the God. v. 4-7
10. Each team member has something to offer. v. 8-11
11. Each team member should be honored and celebrated. {Read: v. 12-27}

{Read: 1 Corinthians 12:28}
1. The team should operate in order. v. 28
2. The **position** {title, office} or **order** {first, second, etc.} within the team doesn't denote importance. v. 28 {Read: 2 Chr. 19:7; Prov. 24:23; Mat. 19:30; 20:1-16}*one is not more important than the other.*

3. Teams are sent & set placed in order by responsibility not rank of importance. v. 28
4. When a team lacks spiritual order it will manifest in natural confusion. v. 28.
5. Every team member is set {ordained} in their order by God not by men. v. 28 {Read: Acts 13:1-4; Gal. 1:15-20}

⇒ C. TEAM LEADERSHIP

{Read: Exodus 6:13}

1. The true leader of every team is God. {Father, Son, Holy Spirit}. v. 13 {Read: Mat. 23:8-12; Acts 13:1-2; Eph. 2:20; 5:23; 1 Pet. 2;25; 5:4; Heb. 3:1}
2. God always places a lead speaker within every team. v. 13 {Read: Acts 13:1-2}
3. The team lead is the one that charges and sends the rest of the team. v. 13.
4. The team lead must know the plan of God to bring the people out of bondage and into there destined promises. v. 13

{Read: Matthew 23:11-12}

1. Team leaders must poses humility and servitude. v. 11-12
2. A leaders greatness are demonstrated by the fruit of humility and service. v. 11-12
3. Team leaders are exalted or demoted by God. v. 12 {Ps. 75: 6-7}

{Read: Luke 22:24-27}

1. Strife can infiltrate the ranks of leadership. v. 22
2. As leaders we must not exercise lordship over the people. v. 25
3. As leaders our authority must not be used to our own benefit. v. 25-26
4. All the members of the team are all equal. v. 26
5. The members of each team must have a spirit of servitude. v. 27
6. The leadership of Christ is the model that each team leader should follow. v. 27

{Read: Acts 6:2-4}

1. All leadership must work together when dealing with church issues. v. 2 {Read: 2 Cor. 6:1}
2. Team leadership must be apt in problem solving. v. 2
3. Leadership must not leave the word of God to solve problems, but they must solve the problem through the word of God. v. 2
4. Though leaders should posses servitude, they must also know when, and how they should administer their service. v. 2
5. Team leadership must understand they cannot do everything. v. 2
6. Team leaders must know how to delegate authority. v. 3
7. As leaders we must look for spirit filled believers with a life of honesty {integrity} when choosing others to lead. v. 3
8. Team leaders must give themselves over to {submit to} prayer and the ministry of the word of God. v. 4

{Read: Acts 10:25-29}

1. No one in leadership should be worshipped. v. 25 {Read: Rev. 19:10}
2. True leadership will not allow worship to come to them. v. 25
3. True leaders realize that they are only men. v. 26
4. True team leaders will destroy the boundaries of prejudice in their teams and the people the team are called to. v. 26-29

{Read: Acts 13:1-4}

1. Each team member is a leader and should be respected as such. v. 1 {Read: Acts 11:30; 14:23; 15: 2, 4, 6, 22-23; 16:4; 20:17, 28; 21:18; Phil. 1:1; 1 Tim. 5:17; Titus 1:5; Jas. 5:14; 1 Pet. 5:1-2} *Plural Eldership.
2. Teams are small mobilized parts of the body of Christ that are lead by the Holy Spirit through man. v.1-2
3. Team leaders must know how to minister to the Lord on a daily basis. v. 1
4. Fasting must be a daily part of team leadership. v. 1 *denying of ones self.
5. There will be certain leaders that will be handpicked by the Holy Spirit to spear head the rest of the team but this does NOT mean they are the greatest. v. 2
6. Before leaders are sent or before they send, prayer and fasting must be initiated. v. 3
7. The laying on of hands is very important in leadership, for it represents a form of release, {impartation of authority, blessing, etc.}. v. 3 {Read: 1 Tim. 4:14; 5:12}
8. Leadership that is not sent to or placed with a team by God the team will see certain ruin. v. 4 {Read: Acts 16:6-7}

{Read: Acts 16:6-10}

1. The leader of the team must go where the Holy Spirit directs them. v. 6-8
2. The team leader must have vision in order to produce direction for the team. v. 9
3. Team leaders must be obedient to the voice of the Lord, to assure team effectiveness. v. 10

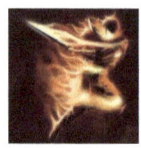

II. TYPES OF TEAMS

⇒ INTERCESSORY TEAMS

Intercession: Entreaty in favor of another, **especially a prayer or petition** to God in behalf of another. **Mediation in a dispute**.

There are two types of intercessory teams: **Covering Intercessors** and **Undergirding Intercessors**. A fine example of this theory can be clearly seen through *Seraphims*, whose position is *above* {*covered*} the throne of God, and *Cheribums*, whose position is *under* {*under girded*} the throne of God. {Is. 6:1-7} *Satan was part of the *Covering Intercessor* team he was a Cheribum {Read: Ezek. 28:14-15} **Covering** deals with the **outward** that is seen, **Undergirding** deals with the **inward** issues which are not seen.

{Read: Judges 7:2-8}

1. Intercessory teams are placed in a region, to intercede {*fight*} for it and its people. v. 1-8
2. Every intercessory team should have a chief intercessor, who is able to receive from God plans, directions, orders, etc. v. 1-8 {*Gideon*}
3. Intercessory teams are usually small and unpopular. v. 1-8
4. Intercessory teams do not have to be large to be effective. v. 1-8
5. Intercessory teams are birthed to fight battles within battles. v. 1-8
6. Intercessory teams are the support system of any army {church} sent to establish the kingdom of God and advance its people. v. 1-8
7. Intercessors and their teams must be careful that they do not fall into vanity, or pride due to victorious battles. v. 2
8. Intercessory teams are to walk, pray and live a life of humility. v. 2
9. God saves entire nations through the vehicle of intercessory teams. v. 2, 7
10. Intercessors must discern throughout the teams who are the bold and who are the fearful. v.3
11. Those that are fearful {*capable of causing fear*} or afraid {*filled with fear*} must be delivered before becoming a part of any intercessory team. v. 3
12. God chooses who should and should not be on the intercessory team and then reveals them to the head intercessor. v. 4
13. Intercessors and their teams must walk in total obedience to the commands they receive from God, no matter how odd or strange they may seem. v. 5-22
14. Music plays and vital part in the role and life of an intercessor. v. 8 {*praise*: the empty pitchers and trumpets & *worship*: the lamps and words uttered} {Read: v. 17-18; Gen. 49:8; Josh. 6:1-26; *1 Sam. 16:14-23;18:10*}
15. Effective intercession will cause the enemy to turn on his own. v. 22 {Read: Gen. 49}
16. Effective intercessory teams open regions for the believer to reap the spoils of a God given victory. v. 22-25

{Read: Psalms 32:5-6}

1. Intercessors and their teams must possess an active and consistent prayer life. v. 5
2. Before intercessors pray for others they must first pray for themselves. v. 5-6 {Read: Jn. Chp. 17}

3. The spirits of confession and repentance should be a continuous act in the life of a intercessor. v. 5-6
4. Sin and/or transgression in the life of the intercessor {believer} hinders one to intercede effectively for someone else. v. 5-6 {Read: Ps. 24:3-4}
5. Intercessory teams must intercede {pray} within the timing of God. v. 6 {Read: Ps. 63:1; Prov. 8:17; Ecc. 3:1-8; Is. 26:9; Jer. 7:16; Mat. 7:7}

{Read: Isaiah 53:12}

1. Intercessory teams take on the spirit of Christ as He IS, not just as He was or shall be. v. 12 {Read: Rom. 8:34; Heb. 7:25}
2. The true intercessory teams pray {pour out} of their soul. v. 12
3. The intercessory team bares the transgressions of many. v.12
4. Intercessory teams intercedes for, and are counted among the transgressors. v. 12
5. Intercession has its rewards. v. 12
6. Intercessory teams reap and divide {share} the spoils {rewards} of their labor. v.12

{Read: Jeremiah 7:16}

1. Intercessory teams must know when to pray and when not to pray, who to pray for and who not to pray for. v. 16
2. God will NOT hear intercession for those who WANT to continue in sin. v. 16 {Read: v. 1-16}

{Read: Ezekiel 9:1-11}

1. Intercessors and their teams are ones who have been given charge over and or burdens for their individual cities. v. 1
2. Intercessory teams possess weapons of destruction. v. 1 {see chapter on team weapons}
3. Intercessory teams must be frequent visitors of the altar. v. 2
4. The altar is where intercessors receive their instructions, empowerment, and bring their gifts {weapons} for maintenance. v. 2 *See weapons maintenance.*
5. Intercessory teams should posses within their teams one who records {writes} the oracles of God. v. 3, 11 * See Scribe teams*
6. Intercessory scribes are given authority to mark {put in memory, write down through spiritual discernment} those that God has divine protection over. In other words the dos and don'ts during intercession. v. 4, 6 {Read: Jer. 7:1-16; 14:7-10}
7. Intercessory teams must be careful that they do not fight against what God has instructed them not to. v. 4
8. Intercessory teams show no pity during prayer unless instructed by God. v.5
9. The power and results of an effective intercessory team are of no respect of person, and begin within the household of faith. v. 6
10. Intercessory teams are released to *pray for* protection, victory and deliverance from the enemy and mercy for pending judgment. v.8 {Read: Ps. 18:47-50; Gen. 18:20-32}

{Read: Ezekiel 22:30}

1. Intercessory teams are sought out by God. v. 30
2. Intercessory teams are ones that make hedges of protection. v. 30
3. Intercessory teams take a stand in the gap that separates the dead and the living, heaven and earth, God and His people. v. 30 {Read: 1 Tim. 2:5}
4. Intercessory teams can stop pending destruction. v. 30
5. Intercessory teams are hard to find. v.30
6. Intercession is for others. v. 30 {Read: 59:16}
7. Intercessory teams stand in the gap to release salvation, righteousness and the sustaining power of God. v. 30. {Read: 59:16}
8. While in the gap, intercessors must have on the full armor of God. v. 30 {Read: 59:17; Eph. 6:11-18}

{Read: Acts 12:5-16}

1. There are two classes of Intercessory teams: *heavenly* and *earthly*. v. 5, 7 {Read: Ezek. 9:1, 8} *See section for *Charge to Angels*.
2. Both *heavenly and earthly* intercessory teams act on the behalf of both God and man. v.5, 7 {Read: Jer. 7:1-16; 14:7-10}
3. The prayers of earthly intercessors, activate and release heavenly intercessors. v. 5-7
4. Heavenly intercessors carry out there assignments until they are fulfilled. v. 7-10
5. Heavenly intercessory teams are released to *execute* {carry out} judgment, and provide protection. v. 7-11 {Read: Ezek. 9: 1-7}
6. Intercessory teams, heavenly or earthly, cause those that are bound to be free. v. 11
7. Intercessory teams must be in total agreement, for this allows their prayers to be manifested right before their eyes. v. 12
8. Those teams with a true hart of intercession will see miraculously answered prayers. v. 12-16
9. Intercessory teams must be aware of unbelief within the ranks. v. 12-16
10. Unbelief can cause intercessory teams to push the fruit of their intercession away. v. 12-16
11. Intercessors must posses the ability to hear the answers of their prayers. v. 12-16

{Read: Romans 8:26-27}

1. The intercessory teams weakness {*infirmity*} often times is the lack of knowledge, understanding and faintheartedness v. 26
2. Intercessory teams don't know what to pray for all of the time. v. 26
3. Intercessory teams must know that it is not them praying but the HOLY SPIRIT praying through them. v. 26
4. There are groans and moans inside the spirit of the intercessor and its teams that only can be released by the Holy Ghost. v. 26 * *Mans extremity is God's opportunity*.
5. The intercessory team receives insight by the Holy Spirit. As the Holy Spirit searches the hearts of men and matches it with the mind of Christ, He then begins to intercede according to the will of God, using the intercessor as a vehicle. v. 27

⇒ GOVERNMENTAL INTERCESSION

Governmental Intercession is interceding for governments. G.I. can only be effective when done with *wisdom* and *understanding* within the power and authority allotted to the individuals. One must take their prayers aim and then launch them towards a target in order to effect that particular area. {Read: 1 Cor. 9:26} Below is a outline of our government and how it is ran that you might be able to target your prayers more effectively concerning your neighborhoods, communities, cities, states and the nation. {Read: 1 Tim. 2:1-5}

FEDERAL GOVERNMENT
The structure and responsibilities of the federal government were defined by the constitution. The federal government's role has been expanded this the Constitution was first written. This expanded role is defined in the Amendments to the Constitution.
The federal government consists of 3 branches:

- Executive Branch
- Legislative Branch
- Judicial Branch

The Executive Branch consists of the *President, Vice President*, executive departments and independent agencies. It is responsible for enforcing the laws of the United States.
The Legislative Branch, or Congress, consists or the Senate *and House of Representatives*. The Legislative Branch is responsible for making the laws which govern the country.

The Judicial Branch consists of the federal courts such as the *Supreme Court, Court of Claims, Court of Customs, Circuit Courts of Appeals and District Courts.* They are responsible for interpreting the laws and ensuring that the rights or the people are protected.

STATE GOVERNMENT
The state government is based on the Constitution. The Constitution states that any powers not specifically given to the federal government are the responsibility of the state. The details of a state government's structure and responsibilities are defined by state constitutions. The state constitutions differ from state to state, but they are all similar to, and do not contradict the U.S. Constitution.

Like the federal government, the state government also has three branches:
- Executive Branch
- Legislative Branch
- Judicial Branch

`**The Executive Branch** is headed by the *Governor*. The *governor* and *advisors* are responsible for carrying out the laws passed by the legislative branch, and are also responsible for proposing new laws.

The Legislative Branch consists of the *State House of Representatives* and *the State Sena*te. They are responsible for making laws that relate to state matters.

The Judicial Branch consists of a hierarch of courts including the *State Supreme Court, Appellate Courts, District Courts* and *Municipal Courts*. State courts hear cases relating to state law. They are responsible for explaining the laws, applying the laws, settling disagreements and deciding who is guilty of breaking a state law.

LOCAL GOVERNMENT
The local government IS NOT based directly on the U.S. Constitution. *The state government* creates a Charter which defines the structure and responsibilities of the local government. It may define several forms of local government such as *city* and *county* governments.

The local government is responsible for administering local programs such as *police* and *fire services, public health and safety, building and repairing roads, collecting garbage, maintaining schools, collecting local and state taxes, running elections, and keeping official marriage and birth records.*

⇒ PRAYER TIPS & TACTICS

Who to Pray For
{Arenas of Executive, Judicial, Legislative}

1. **Political Arena**:
{Presidents, Prime Ministers, Dictators, Ambassadors,
Political Advisors, Governors, Senators, Majors, etc.}
2. **Judicial Arena**:
{Judges, Court, Law Enforcement}
3. **Spiritual Arena**:
{All Spiritual Leaders *gifts* and *offices*}
4. **Educational Arena**:
{Teachers, Professors, Etc.}
5. **Cultural Arena**:
{Entertainment Industry, The Arts, Sports, Etc.}
6. **Commercial Arena**:
{Advertising, Radio, Television, Newspaper, Corporate Executives}

7. Civic Arena:
{Those responsible for the health and morality of the community}
8. Social Arena:
{Social Groups, half way houses, homeless shelters, county offices, social services, etc.}
9. The Local Church:
{Vision, Unity, Growth and Expansion}
10. The Body of Christ:
{Restoration, Unity, Vision, Growth and Expansion}

⇒ What to Pray Against

1. Governmental Strongholds
2. Cultural Strongholds
3. Religious Strongholds
4. Material {worldly} Strongholds

⇒ What to Pray For

1. Leaders will do justly, govern truthfully with a spirit of sincerity.
2. Love mercy-govern compassionately with a spirit of generosity.
3. Walk humbly– govern modestly with a spirit of sensitivity to God.
4. That leaders would repent, submit and reverence God.
5. That leaders would recognize and acknowledge God in all that they do.
6. Receive a personal message of God's love.
7. That leaders would grow weary of shedding innocent blood.
8. Pray that leaders would repent and turn there hearts would turn to the Lord.
9. That God would give the leaders love, humility, wisdom, discernment, and righteous judgment.
10. That corrupt leaders will fall from power and just leaders put in place.
11. Fear of the Lord would return in the nations and churches.

⇒ Postures of Prayer

1. **Bowing:** *Bent over {Gen. 24:26; Ex. 4:31}
2. **Knelling:** *On your knees{1 Kin. 8:45; Acts 7:60; 9}
3. **Prostrate:** *On your face {Num. 20:6; Mat. 26:39}
4. **Standing:** *On your feet{1 Kin. 8:22; Mk. 11:25}
5. **Sitting:** *On your buttocks {1 Chr. 17:16-27}
6. **Hands Uplifted:** * In all positions above{1 Tim. 2:8}

⇒ Plateaus of Prayer

1. **Lepers** *Speaking to God (Confessions)
2. **Priestly** *Speaking with God (Conversation)
3. **Sonship** *Speaking for God (Declaring)
3. **Kingly** *Speaking as God (Decreeing)

⇒ <u>Components of Prayer</u>
1. Intercession: {Ja. 5:13-16}
2. Adoration: {Dan. 4:34-35}
3. Confession: {1 Jn. 1:9}
4. Thanksgiving: { Phil. 4:6}
5. Supplication: {1 Tim. 2:1-3}

⇒ SCOUTING TEAMS

<u>Scout</u>: **A person who explores new territories**: {i.e. pioneer, settler, explorer}; **To spy on or explore carefully in order to obtain information**; reconnoiter; **One that is dispatched from a main body to gather information, especially in preparation for military action**; The act of reconnoitering; **A watcher or sentinel**.

{Read: Joshua 2:1-24}

1. Before a region {area} is invaded, scouting teams must be sent out. v. 1-2
2. The number of scouts sent can be related to how vast the region is. v.1 {Read: Num. Chp. 13-14, the governmental *twelve men* into Canaan}
3. Scouting teams are made up of spies that are highly trained agents sent to gather information on the region that will be invaded {*Spiritual mapping*: i.e. manpower, defenses and fertility, etc.}. v. 1
4. Scouting teams are usually hand picked, trained, and sent by the team leader {i.e. Moses, Joshua}. v. 1-2 {Read: Num. 13:1-3,17}
5. King David as well as Jesus had scouting teams. v. 1 {Read: 1 Sam. 26:4; Lk. 9:51-53}
6. Scouting teams must possess keen eyesight {*spiritual discernment*} in order to assess the region. v. 1 {Read: Num. 13:18}
7. Scouting teams should be trained to be quick to listen, and slow to speak {key words: spy secretly}. v. 1 {Read: 1 Thes. 4:11; Jam. 1:19} *see chapter on " Entering a Region"*
8. Without scouting teams it would be very difficult to successfully **enter**, **attack** and **overtake** a region. v. 1 -2 {Read: Num. 21:1}
9. God provides what we call safe houses, {spiritual and natural} to hide the teams that are sent out. v. 1-6 {Read: Lk. 9:4}
10. Our enemy is very aware of scouting teams and their spies, so he will send search parties to flush the team out of their positions. v. 2, 16
11. Scouting teams have people within each reason designed to help them to learn the land. {i.e. Rahab} v. 1-22 {Read: Acts 18:9-10; Heb. 11:31; Jam. 2:25}
12. Scouting teams are to bring reports back to the team leader. v.23-24

{Read: Num. 13:1-3,17-20}

1. To qualify for the scouting teams, one must be a faithful and experienced leader. v. 2
2. The scouting teams are usually sent from the headquarters location that is encamped around outskirts of the targeted area. * Sent FROM Paran TO spy out Canaan. v. 3
3. The scouting team must be able to receive and follow the instructions. v.17
4. Scouting teams should be sent strategically into the land. v. 17 * *southward, go into the mountain.*
5. Scouting teams assess the strength, weakness, and number of the enemy. v. 18
6. Scouting teams assess the land for building and battling purposes. v. 18, 20
7. Scouting teams assess the strength of the enemy's buildings {encampments}. v. 18

- **Tents**, easy to pull {throw} down, root up {pluck up} and set fire to.
- **Strongholds** a siege must be laid predicated upon the strength of the stronghold. Strongholds must be broken down and destroyed which could take the battle into overtime.
- **Kingdom Institutions**– are strengthened strongholds that have broaden its reach into other city-states. Kingdom Institutions have an educational, judicial and financial system set in place. At this stage a greater strategy is needed to gain entrance to take down its government. {Ref Jer. 1:10; 31:28; Ezek. 4:1-6}

8. Scouting teams must bring back proof of their journey into the land. v. 20 *the bushel of grapes.*
9. Scouting teams must possess courage. v. 20
10. Scouting teams are the first to see what enemy inhabits the land up close and personal. v. 20
11. Scouting teams were not designed for hand on hand combat, they fight with there eyes, but they should possess fighting ability in case they are placed in that position. {Read: Num. 21:1}
12. Scouting teams are the eyes of the rest of the team, through their eyes of faith we must be able see victory. {Read: Num. 13:30; 14:6-9}

SCOUTING TEAM EXERCISE

Develop a **scouting team by gathering people** who will volunteer their time to **gather information** about the region (location, community, city, etc.) from **social media sites** and **stations, news papers**, and or **word of mouth**. These scouting teams must be passionate about recognizance missions. Send the team out to gather and when they come back provide this information to your **intercessory teams** and begin to target these areas until you see break through. You can have more than one scouting team with a suggested **2-5** members, depending on the size of your ministry. **Keep a record** of your regions process by **developing graphs** and **charts** to share with the rest of your ministry to encourage them in their pursuit of regional restoration.

⇒ MINSTREL TEAMS

Minstrel: a musician; a *bard*; a singer. *bard*: a tribal *poet*-singer skilled in composing and reciting verses on heroes and their deeds b : a composer, singer, or declaimer of epic or heroic verse.

{Read: Genesis 49:8}

1. When the minstrel team plays their music it literally takes the form of a hand and chokes the enemy. v. 8

{Read: Num. 18:6-7}

1. The gift of the minstrel comes from the line of Levi and is consider a gift FOR God given TO the Body of Christ for the service of His house {*tabernacle*} and His people {*congregation*}. v. 6-7
2. The minstrel is an essential part of the Levitical Priesthood, for they are hand picked by God. v. 6-7
3. The minstrel team mustn't view themselves as just musicians, but they must know, understand and walk as the *musical priest* they were called out to be. v. 7
4. The minstrel holds the office of a priest while exercising the gift of song, poetry, writing and prophecy. v. 7
5. The minstrel team must have a consistent prayer life. v. 7
6. The minstrel team must know that their office and talents are gifts from God. v. 7
7. The minstrel team must go beyond the veil into the very presence of God to better serve God, His people to execute His purposes. v. 7

{Read: Judges 7:21-22}

1. The minstrel team's music surrounds and confuses the enemy. v. 21
2. The minstrel team's music puts the devil on the run. v. 21, 22
3. The minstrel team's music serves as a camouflage, that actually makes the enemy believe that there are more of us than it is of him. v. 21
4. The music of the minstrel team can cause the enemy to destroy his own. v. 22

{Read: 1 Chronicles. 15:22, 27}

1. When dealing with the *minstrel team* there must be a **sent-set minstrel**, one set in place to be the *master of the song* {a chief psalmist, head musician, worship leader etc.} to spearhead the other minstrels of the team in the correct way of handling the presence of the Lord. {*Chenaniah, David*} v. 22

2. A **master minstrel** and their *team* posses a supernatural ability to instruct {teach} through their music. v. 22 {Read: Col. 3:16}{*Hebrew* word for *instruct*: **yacar**- *to chastise literally with blows or figuratively with words to bind, chasten, correct, punish, reform, reprove, sore, teach*}

    a.) *Dealing with the believer* the minstrel and their music sends forth an impartation of knowledge {teaching} that comforts, edifies, corrects, reforms, reproves, and even disciplines {chastises} the believer.

    b.) *Dealing with the enemy*, or even spirits the believer might have, the minstrel teams music throws fighting blows in the spirit with the melody, and power of the song, while the words of the song binds the enemy, giving the captive a chance to be free.

3. Minstrels and their teams must possess *robes* of fine *linen* {the correct garment}, which serves as mantles {*spirits*} of purity. In other words *their spirits must be pure*. v. 27 **Robes**= *Hebrew* word is *mehel*: in the sense of covering, cloke, coat, *and mantle*. **Linen**= *Hebrew* word is *buwts*: to bleach, to be *white*, fine *white* linen. *white represents purity*.

4. Minstrel teams MUST walk in holiness. v. 27 {Read: Num. 8:6-7, 21}

{Read: 1 Chr. 25:1}

1. God empowers minstrel and uses men to release them. v. 1
2. Minstrel teams are designed to move prophetically within the service {battle}. v. 2
3. Minstrels release an atmosphere conducive for deliverance and the word of the Lord. v.1 {Read: 2 Kin. 3:15}
4. All minstrels posses the creative ability to prophesy in word, song and music. v. 1 {Read: 1 Chr. 25:2}* This statement DOES NOT mean that all minstrels are *PROPHETS,* this simply means that they may be operating under the *SPIRIT* of prophecy or posses the *GIFT* of prophecy} {Read: Num. 11:26-30; 1 Cor. 13:2}
5. Minstrel teams should be skilled in area of the prophetic. v.1 {Read: 1 Chr. 15:22}
6. The prophetic music of the minstrel team assists in the proclamation of Gods word. v. 1
7. The minstrels music proceeds, carries and assists the word of the Lord, it breaks through demonic atmospheres. v. 1 {Read: Jud. 7:16-20; 1 Kin. 1:40}
8. Minstrel teams are birthed through the prophetic. v. 1 {Read: v.5; Ex. 7:1; Num. 18:1; 1 Chr. 16:42; 25:4; 2 Chr. 29:25}
9. Minstrel teams activate the prophetic within people, especially leadership. v. 1 {Read: 2 Kin. 3:15}
10. Minstrels are types of musical PRIESTS that carry a prophetic anointing. v. 1 {Read: Gen. 29:34; 46:11, * **Levi**– *Joined*; {Read: Num. 18:1-7), ***Aaron**-meaning uncertain* 1 Chr. 15:22, * **Chenaniah**- *Jehovah has chosen*; {Read: 1 Chr. 1:3}, ***Jeduthan**-The praising one*; 1 Chr. 25:2, ***Aspah**-Jehovah has gathered*; {1 Chr. 16:42; 25:4-5}, ***Heman**– Faithful*

{Read: 1 Chr. 25:6}

1. Every minstrel team should be submitted to a higher authority to operate effectively within their callings. v. 6

{Read: 2 Chr. 20:22}

1. Minstrel teams should minister to the Lord before going into battle. v. 21 **Give Him praise for the beauty of His holiness*. {Jn. 12:32}
2. Minstrel teams are on the front line of battle, they lead the army. v. 21
3. Minstrel teams release the Lords ambushes against the enemy. v. 22

{Read: 2 Chr. 23:1-18}

1. Minstrel teams are chosen to protect leadership. v. 1-2
Minstrel teams should be in a covenant agreement with the leadership to protect the people and the king at all costs. v. 3 {Read: Amos. 3:3}
3. Minstrel teams should strategically set up themselves as a supernatural barrier that surrounds the leader to fight off and demonic attacks. v. 4-10 {Read: 1 Sam. 16:14-23}
4. Minstrel teams are apostolic, they are called and sent by God. v. 2-4 {Read: Num. 1:50-53; 3:6-9; 4:1-33; Mk. 2:14; Lk. 5: 27-29, *Levi-Matthew*}

{Read: Mat. 9:23}

1. Minstrel teams fight against the effects of death. v. 23

In closing, keep this in mind, **Jeduthun** *was the father of* **Obed-Edom** {Read: 1 Chr. 16:38} Obed-Edom was a gatekeeper and a host of God's presence. He was one who helped transport the ark of the covenant to Jerusalem, and also a guardian of the sacred vessels in the temple. {Read: 1 Chr. 15:18-24; 26:4, 8, 15; 2 Chr. 25:24} Therefore, keeping in line with our topic **minstrel teams** we can glean some valued lessons and tactics when implementing minstrel teams.

⇒ Minstrel teams are prophetic musical priesthood that birth the kingdom of Heaven and of God.
⇒ Minstrel teams release a supernatural anointing of protection that invites, surrounds and safeguards the

presence of the Lord and His people.
- ⇒ Minstrels make **melody** within their hearts to the Lord, while their **message** goes to the people.
- ⇒ Minstrel also carry and release the voice of the bride and bridegroom. {songs of the Lord and His bride} into the region.
- ⇒ Minstrels host and transport God's presence.
- ⇒ Choirs are part of the minstrel teams Ezra had 200 voice choir and Nehemiah had 245.

*Without the proper training and releasing of minstrel teams, our ministries and regions, will be desolate.
{Ez. 2:65; Neh. 7:67; Jer. 7:34; 16:9; 25:10, 33:11; Eph. 5:19; Col. 3:16 Rev. 18:23}

⇒ EVANGELISM TEAMS

Evangelism: **1**. the winning or revival of personal commitments to Christ. **2** militant or crusading zeal. **Proclaiming the gospel to those who haven't heard it**. There are two classes of evangelism.

First class is sent to the **church** {the religious arena} *Stephen* Acts 6:1-13; Eph., 4:11-16
The **second** is sent to the **unsaved** {the secular arena}. *Philip* Acts 8:1-12

{Read: Acts 6: 1-13}

1. Evangelists and their teams are an extension of {stem from} the deaconhood. (place of servitude) v. 1-5 {Read: Acts 21:8}
2. Evangelists and their teams posses the qualities of the deacon {server}. v. 1-5 {Read: 1 Tim. 3:8-13}
3. Evangelism teams should be birthed by true evangelists. v. 5 * *Stephen and Philip*
4. Evangelism team members MUST be filled with the Holy Ghost and wisdom. v. 3
5. Evangelism teams are called to address the spiritual and natural needs of the people. v. 1-3
6. Evangelism teams are empowered by apostolic prayer. v. 6
7. Evangelism teams are **set** and **sent** by apostles. v. 6
8. Evangelists and their teams should be full of the word of God. v. 7
9. Evangelists and their teams posses the power of multiplication {increase}. v. 7
10. Evangelists and their teams face much resistance, especially from legalistic, religious and witchcraft spirits. v. 12
11. Lying spirits are sent out to destroy the ministry of the evangelists. v. 13

{Read: Acts 8: 1-12}

1. Evangelism teams are formed by the fires of persecution and hardships. v. 1-4 {Read: 2 Tim. 4:5}
2. Evangelism teams break through geographical, denominational and cultural barriers. v. 1
3. The evangelism team's message must be authoritative, powerful and simple. v. 5
4. Evangelism teams posses the gift of miracles. v. 6
5. Evangelism teams cast out devils. v. 7
6. Evangelism teams bring great joy to a city. v. 8
7. Evangelism teams baptize in the water {word} and make way for the baptism of the Spirit. v. 12 {Read: Acts 8:1-12; Eph. 5:26}
8. Evangelism teams preach and demonstrate the word of the Lord. v. 6 {Read: Rom. 15:18}
9. Evangelism teams not only allow the lost to hear the word but they allow the word to be seen in action. v. 6
10. One of the chief enemies of evangelism team is that of witchcraft, mainly charismatic, fuelled by religious spirits. v. 8-9
11. Evangelism teams posses the power to break the power of the witchcraft and deception {sorcery}. v. 9-11
12. Evangelism teams are to preach the things concerning the kingdom of God and the name of Jesus Christ, NOT the ministries they are from. v. 12
13. Evangelism teams turn regions upside down. v. 12 {Read: Acts 17:6}
14. As evangelism teams preach and demonstrate the word of God the blood of Christ is applied. v. 12 {Read: Acts 5:28}
15. Evangelism teams walk in signs and wonders. v. 13 {Read: Chp. 6:8; Rom. 15:19}
16. Evangelism teams are sent to prepare the way for apostles. v. 14

{Read: Acts 21: 8-9}

1. Evangelist's and their teams should posses a spirit of hospitality. v. 8
2. Evangelist's and their teams can activate prophecy. v. 9
3. Evangelism teams attract and draw from the anointings of apostles and prophets.

{Read: Romans 15:18-22}

1. Evangelists, nor their teams, must not do anything outside the boundaries of Christ to win people to. v. 18
2. Evangelism teams should be sent to uncharted territories, people and nations. v. 20 * *Where the TRUE JESUS CHRIST has not yet been preached.* [Read: Acts 17:6]
3. When the TRUE Christ is being preached the geographical location and its inhabitants are effected {changed}. v. 20 {Read: Acts 17:6}
4. Evangelism teams should not be limited to the evangelist, but embraced by the entire five fold ministry. v. 20 {Read: Rom. 1:1} *The gift and or spirit of evangelism can flow throughout every believer.*
5. Evangelism teams should not go beyond their prescribed territory. v. 20 {Read: 2 Cor. 10:13-16}

{Read: Ephesians 3:17-19}

1. The message of the evangelism team should take root in the heart of the hearer and then make them grounded in love. v. 17
2. The message of the evangelism team should reach the full spectrum of the region, and its people. v. 18-19 (see diagrams on page 59)

    - **Breadth**-*width:*   Distance from side to side. {Is. 8:8}

      Hebrew– *Merchab*: Open space, liberty; *Rachab*: width, expanse.
      Greek– *Platos*: width

    - **Length**- Distance from one place to another. {Acts 1:8}

      Hebrew– *Achariyth*: future; *Orek*: length {Rev. 21:16}
      Greek– *Mekos*– length; *Pote*: at the some time, ever.

    - **Depth**- Distance downward.

      Hebrew– *Amaq*: to be, make deep. {Mk. 4:5, 16-17; 2 Cor. 12:7; Eph. 3:17}
      Greek– *Bathos*: extent mystery. {Eph. 3:3}

    - **Height**   Distance from the bottom to the top of something.

      Hebrew– *Gabahh/Gobahh:* to be lofty, haughty-arrogant, powerful, high*; Marrowm*: elevation, elation; *Rosh*: head; *Ruwm*: altitude, tallness {Read: Rev. 21:16}; Ramuwth: heap of carcasses.
      Greek– Hupsos: altitude, sky; dignity; Hupsoma– altitude barrier. {Read: Rev. 21:16}

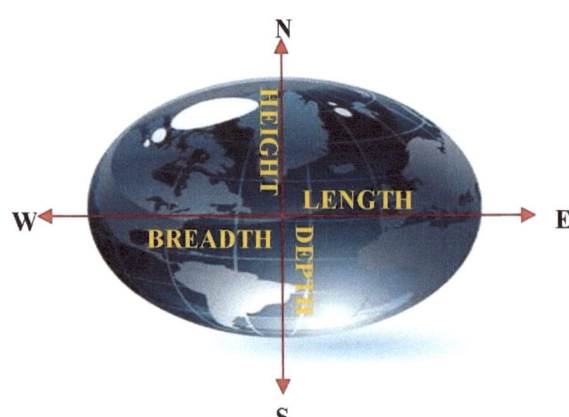

3. When true evangelism has been wrought, the totality of the CROSS should have been ministered, **N**orth **E**ast **W**est **S**outh. {proclaiming the good **news**}
4. Evangelism teams message effect the **earth realm** and the **spiritual realm**. v. 18
5. True evangelism Produce a **horizontal** and **vertical** effect.

{**horizontal**– *breadth* & *length*- **earth realm**: the world and it's people}
{**vertical**– *height* & *depth*- **spiritual realm**: heaven, hell and their inhabitants}
{Read: Jn. 12:32; Mat. 16:18}

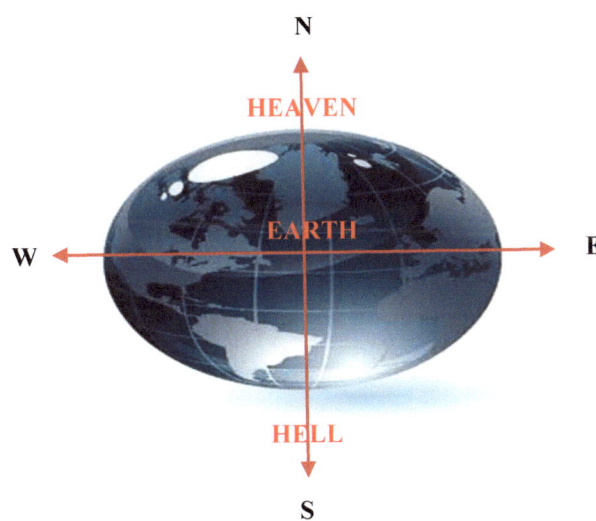

5. Evangelism teams know when their message has effected **heaven** and **hell**, for God opens the heavens and pours out His spirit and hell gives over its captives {people are set free}, and come to the Lord. {Read: Lk. 15:7-10; Acts 2:4; 18:5-8 }

⇒ DELIVERANCE TEAMS

Deliverance: the **act of delivering** someone or something; **the state of being delivered**; *especially*: liberation, rescue; something delivered; *especially*; an opinion or decision (as the verdict of a jury) expressed publicly. * Note: *most deliverance teams are made up of a lead, intercessor, and a helper, but are not limited to this structure, for their roles can switch at any given time. {i.e. the helper can take lead or intercede, etc.* Acts 13:5}

{Read: Genesis 45:7}

1. We must be called and then sent to do deliverance. v. 7
2. Deliverance has a power to preserve. v. 7

{Read: 2 Kings 5:1}

1. You can do deliverance and still need it yourself. v. 1
2. Deliverance teams must live honorable lives. v. 1
3. Deliverance teams must be submitted under authority. v. 1
4. Deliverance teams must be men and women of valor {*bravery, courage, intrepidity, prowess in war*}. v. 1

{Read: Psalms 44:1-7}

1. Deliverance has always been here, it's nothing new. v. 1 {Read: Ecc. 1: 9-10}
2. Deliverance drives out darkness and plants God's light bearers in its place. v. 2
3. Deliverance is not done by our own power, words, or weapons, but by God's spirit. v. 3 {Read: Zech. 4:6; Acts 3:12-16}
4. The favor of God must be upon a person, region, etc. for deliverance to manifest. v. 3
5. The Lord must command the deliverance before it happens. v. 4
6. Deliverance must be sanctioned in heaven before it manifested on earth. v. 4
7. Deliverance pushes down and places the enemy under our feet. v. 5 {Read: Job 40:12}
8. In deliverance we cannot trust in our own weapons or words. v. 6 {Read: Ps. 33:16-17}
9. Deliverance brings shame upon the enemy. v. 7

{Read: 2 Kings 13:17}

1. The prophetic anointing opens up the spirit realm for deliverance teams. v. 17
2. The prayers and words of deliverance teams are like arrows in the spirit. v. 17
3. Deliverance consumes the enemy. v. 17
4. Deliverance teams must follow the voice of the Lord. v. 18
5. Deliverance teams must have prophetic insight {discernment}. v. 18-19

{Read: 1 Chronicles 11:14}

1. Deliverance teams are set up in the midst of the land {region} that is under fire. v. 14

{Read: 2 Chronicles 12:7}

1. Deliverance teams MUST walk in humility, for humility activates deliverance. v. 7
2. Deliverance teams are closely knit to the prophet and/or prophetic teams. v. 7 {Read: 2 Kin. 13:17}
3. Deliverance teams must know that people, regions, etc. may not always receive total deliverance through their work. v. 7 {Deut. 7:22}

{Read: Ezra 9:13}

1. Deliverance teams are sent forth due to the increase of sin in a region. {evil, trespass}. v. 13
2. Deliverance teams are placed in a region to keep away the full judgment of God. v. 13

3. Deliverance teams should move in the timing of God. v. 13 *such*: Hebrew word means *keneth*– at such time {Read: Ex. 2:23-25; Est. 4:14}

{Read: Ester 4:14}

1. Deliverance is not limited to one person and/or geographical area. v. 14
2. Deliverance teams mustn't keep quiet when it comes to setting people free. v. 14
3. Deliverance teams bring enlargement to a region. v. 14
4. Entire families, generations can be wiped out if deliverance is silenced and teams aren't trained and released. v. 14

{Read: Psalms 18:50}

1. God gives leaders great deliverance. v. 50
2. Leadership is not exempt from deliverance. v. 50 {Read: 2 Kin. 5:1; Lu. 12:48}
3. Deliverance teams are God's mercy givers. v. 50
4. Deliverance is God's way of giving mercy to His people. v. 50 {Read: Mat. 20:30-34}
5. Deliverance not only effects us, but also our children. v. 50

{Read: Psalms 32:7}

1. Deliverance teams should utilize music to combat the enemy. v. 7
2. Deliverance teams possess a power to preserve {protect} the region and its people from pending trouble. v. 7 * *See Section on Minstrel teams*
3. Deliverance teams can produce prophetic melodies that set up barriers around the region. v. 7
4. Deliverance teams and their songs manifest the Lords hiding places {trenches} for those in trouble. v. 7 {Read: Ps. 61:3; 144:2; Prov. 18:10; Is. 26:20}

{Read: Isaiah 26:18}

1. Deliverance teams are sent where there is a need. v. 18
2. Deliverance teams are spiritual midwifes that help the child {ministry} bearer to give birth. v. 18
3. Deliverance teams help prevent spiritual miscarriages and still born births. v. 18

{Read: Joel 2:32}

1. Deliverance only comes through and by the name of Jesus Christ. v. 32
2. Deliverance teams MUST use the name of Jesus Christ to bring forth TRUE deliverance. v. 32
3. The greatest weapon that the deliverance team has against the enemy is name of JESUS CHRIST. v. 32
4. Deliverance teams are made up of a class of believers that are steadfast and unmovable. v. 32 {Read: Jer. 1:17-18; Rom. 4:20-21; Eph. 2:20; 1 Cor. 15:58} Zion: Hebrew-tsiyuwn {*tsee-yone*} which means as **a permanent capital**; *a* **monumental** *or* **guiding pillar**. *Jerusalem: Hebrew– Yeruwshalayim {*yer-oo-shaw-lah-yim*} founded peaceful, the capital of Palestine.*

{Read: Obadiah 17}

1. Deliverance teams teach, preach, demonstrate and produce holiness where they are sent. v.17
2. Deliverance teams cause the people of the region to posses their possessions. v. 17
3. Deliverance teams must keep perversion out to keep God in. v. 17 {Read: Heb. 12:14}

{Read: Matthew 15:22-28}

1. Deliverance teams CANNOT operate within a spirit of prejudice. v. 22 {Read: v. 22-24; Mk. 7:26; Gal. 3:28}
2. Deliverance goes beyond the traditions and customs of men. v. 22
3. Deliverance teams crush the walls of traditions and customs of men. v. 22
4. Deliverance teams cast out devils. v. 22
5. Deliverance is the children's {believers'} bread. v. 26 {Read: Mk. 1:21}
6. Deliverance teams deliver the bread {manna} to the children. v. 26

7. Deliverance teams not only do deliverance but they speak deliverance. v. 28
8. The word of deliverance has instant effects. v. 28
9. Deliverance teams must realize that faith is a part of the work. v. 28. {Read: Acts 3:16}

{Read: Mark 1:21-27}

1. Deliverance is part of the doctrine of Jesus Christ and His apostles. v. 22, 27
2. Deliverance teams posses strong a teaching anointing. v. 21-22
3. Deliverance teams breaks through and down the wall of tradition, religion, formalism and ceremonialism. v. 21-23
4. Deliverance teams cause demons to speak out when they enter a region. v. 24
5. Deliverance teams carry an authority that demons and unclean spirits obey. v. 27

{Read: Mark 5:1-15}

1. Deliverance teams must be willing to travel. v.1
2. Deliverance teams will sometimes have to clean up other peoples mess in deliverance. v. 3-4
3. Deliverance teams will experience all kinds of weird things when dealing with deliverance. v. 5
4. Deliverance teams should get the people to worship, for worship exposes devils. v. 6

{Read: Mark 7:24-30}

1. Deliverance teams mustn't bring any attention to themselves when entering a region. v. 24
2. Deliverance is a ministry that attracts people. v. 25 {Read: Mk. 1:33}
3. Some people will only receive a little deliverance. v. 28
4. In deliverance be conscience of time not limited by it. Once deliverance is complete, send release the people, so others might come. v. 29
5. Deliverance teams should be able to meet the needs of the people. v. 30

{Read: Luke 9:49-50}

1. Deliverance teams must realize that not all deliverance teams function the same. v. 49
2. Deliverance is a worldwide ministry, its not just limited to a specific team or local ministry. v. 50
3. Anyone that does deliverance is working with Christ and not against Him. v. 50

{Read: Luke 10:17}

1. Deliverance teams must be careful not to let pride come in. v. 17
2. The real joy of the deliverance team is that there names are written in heaven. v. 17
3. Deliverance teams obtain there *authority* over devils and the *power* to cast devils out, through their names being written in heaven. v. 17 {Read: Mark 16:17}

⇒ SCRIBE TEAMS

Scribe: A person who serves as a professional copyist, especially one who made copies of manuscripts before the invention of printing. Also called a sopher, sofer, in Judaism. One of the group of Palestinian scholars and teachers of Jewish law and tradition, active from the 5th Century B.C. to the 1st century A.D. who transcribed, edited and interpreted the bible. Scribes are teachers put in place to help the Body of Christ remember the laws, statues and commandments of God. Scribes (teacher) in Rabbinic circles means to REPEAT. Scribes (teachers) were set in place to 'repeat' the words of God over and over in the peoples hearing to fixate the word of the Lord in the mindset of the people.

Names of Scribes: (but not limited to)

- Ahiah: {Read:1 Kings 4:3} his name means *"my brother is Jehovah"*
- Ahilud: {Read: 2 Samuel 8:16} his name means *"a brother is born"*
- Elihoreph: {Read: 1 Kings 4:3}his name means *"God of harvest rain"*
- Ezra: {Read: Ezra 7:11-12} his name means *"God is a help"*
- Jehoshaphat {Read: 1 Kings 4:3} his name means *"the Lord is judge"*
- Seraiah: {Read: 2 Sam. 8:17} his name means *"solider of the Lord"*.
- Shapan: {Read: 2 Kings 22:3, 8}his name means *"rock badger"*
- Shebna: {Read: 2 Kings 18:18, 32; 19:2} his name means *"to grow or growth"* {fell from power and died due to pride, Isa. 22:15-25}
- Sheva: {2 Sam. 20:25} his name means *"false"*.

{Read: 2 Samuel 8:16-17; 20:25}

1. Scribes and there teams walk very closely with those in leadership.
2. Scribes and there teams should be established within the government of the local church. {Read: Ex 5:6-8}

{Read: 2 Kings 12:10}

1. Scribe teams possess an anointing to handle and record the finances of the ministry. v.10 {Read: 2 Kin. 22:9}

{Read: 2 Kings 18:17, 37}

1. The scribe and their teams are often times the first to hear the plans of the enemy. v. 37
2. The scribe team will be the ones that pen the agendas of the enemy that are extracted through prayer.

{Read: 2 Kings 19:2}
1. Repentance is the mantel of the Scribes . v.2

{Read: 2 Kings 22:3, 8-10}

1. Scribe teams are apostolic, for they are sent. v. 3
2. Scribe teams are sent to the house of God. v. 3
3. Scribes not only write and record the word of the Lord, but they also speak it. v. 8-10

{Read: Ezra 7:6}
1. Scribes are learned in the word of God. v. 6

2. Scribe teams allow the region and its people to experience the favor of God. v.6
3. The hand of the Lord must be upon the scribe team. v. 6

{Read: Jeremiah 36:26, 32}

1. Scribes and there teams are apostolic secretaries that pin the words from the mouths of the leadership with accuracy and precession.
2. Scribes and there teams flow with the prophet that they might pen the prophetic words of the Lord that are coming from the heart of God. * Apostle Paul also utilized scribes to inscribe his teachings, letters etc. {Rom. 16:22; Gal. 6:11; 2 Thes. 3:17}
3. Scribes and there teams are protected {hid} by the Lord to preserve, not only their lives, but their writings.
4. Scribes and there teams restore God sent truths that have been tampered with or destroyed by the enemy.

{Read: Jeremiah 37:15, 20}

1. Scribes and there teams must be careful they do not kill or keep the people of God in bondage. v. 15, 20 * *Legalism, Tradition and Religion study the woes of scribes {Mat. 23; Mk. 12:38; 4:1}*

{Read: Jeremiah 52:25}

1. There should be a principle scribe to provide proper training for scribe teams. v.25
2. Principal scribes have an ability to muster {exhort, gather} the people into a battle. v.25

{Read: Matthew 23:34}

1. Scribes and their teams will be persecuted and killed because of the gospel. v. 24

{Read: Mark 2:6}

1. Scribes must beware of intellectual spirits. v. 6 {Read: Lk. 5:21}

⇒ PROPHETIC TEAMS
{Read: Jud. 4:4; 1 Sam. 3:1, 19-20; Amos 3:7; Joel 2:28-29}

Prophetic teams are made up of up of *Prophets, Prophetess, Seers* and or Holy spirit filled and or inspired people who will speak for God, communicating the message of His heart to a people, nation or land of His choice. **Prophetic teams** are not limited to *gender, age, nor number*, so whenever God wants to speak, do or reveal anything to a people He releases His voice through these teams or individuals. Prophetic teams are extensions of prophetic **schools** and that reside in **colleges**. (2 Ki. 2:3-7; 22:14; 2 Chr.34:22) I personally don't believe a person can be TAUGHT HOW TO PROPHESY, for each individual handles the prophetic differently according to their character, personality and or how God deals with him or her. On the other hand, one can be given understanding on HOW THE PROPHETIC WORKS. Therefore, understanding the workings of the prophetic will enable the individuals or teams to be used more effectively as they prophecy.

Prophetic teams can flow in one or all the manifestations of the prophetic:

The *Spirit of Prophecy*: {Joel 2:28-29; Rev. 19:10}

* The manifestations of the *spirit of prophecy* are **prophecies, dreams, visions** {night/day}, **prophetic demonstration**. {but not limited to}

- The *spirit of prophecy* **rests** {comes} **upon you**
- The *spirit of prophecy* is for our flesh not our spirits. v. 28
- The *spirit of prophecy* needs flesh to operate. v. 28
- The *spirit of prophecy* comes before and or after NATURAL restoration. v. 21-28
- The *spirit of prophecy* can use all flesh. * *the believer or unbeliever* {Read: Ps. 68:18; Rom. 11:29}

{Read: Revelation 19:10}

- Prophetic teams carry humility. v. 10
- The *spirit of prophecy* testifies of Jesus Christ. v. 10
- Those that carry the *spirit of prophecy* should not be worshipped. v. 10

The *Gift of Prophecy* {Rom. 1:11; 1 Cor. 13:2; 14:1-4; Eph. 4:8, 11; 1 Tim. 1:14; 2 Tim. 1:6}

* The manifestations of the *gift of prophecy* are **edification, exhortation, comfort, perfection of the saints, understanding** and **clarity**. {but not limited to}

- The *gift of prophecy* is **given to you** by God and or through the laying on of hands.
- The *gift of prophecy* can flow within all of the manifestations of prophecy.
- The *gift of prophecy* can be given or stirred by the laying on off hands. {Read: Rom. 1:1; 2 Tim. 1:6}
- All forms of the prophetic can be controlled, quenched or despised {Read: 1 Cor. 14:32; 1 Thes. 5:19-20}
- Other ministry gifts/teams can be given the gift of prophecy. {Read: Amos 1:1; 7:14-13; 1 Cor. 12:11}

The **Office of the Prophet** {the official prophet} {Read: Jer. 1:5; Lk. 1:13-16}

* The manifestations of the *Official Prophet are:* **root**ing out, **pull**ing and **throw**ing down, **destroy**ing, **afflict**ing, **pluck**ing up, **build**ing and **plant**ing. (Read: Jer. 1:10; 18:7-10; 24:6; 31:28}

- An *official prophet* is **who** and or **what God made you** before birth.
- Everything about a *official prophet* is prophetic.
- An official prophet envelopes both the spirit and gift of the prophetic.
- An official prophet is the fullness of prophetic grace.

The **spirit, gift** and **office of the prophetic** all can flow in the **Prophetic Arts**

The *Song* of the Lord. (*Bride & Groom*)
{Jer. 16:9; 25:10; 33:11-14; Eph. 5:19; Col 3:16}

The *Dance* of the Lord.
{Ex. 15:19-20; 2 Sam. 6:14; Ps. 149:3; 150:4}

Prophetic *Flags & Banners*
{***Flags***: Num. 1:52-53; 2:1-34; Jer. 4:6, 21; 50:2; 51:12; Is. 49:22; 62:10}
{***Banners***: Ps. 20:5; 60:4; Sol. 2:4; 6:4; Is. 13:2}

⇒ APOSTOLIC PRESBYTERIES

Apostolic: Of the apostles order, traits, character and lifestyle. **Presbyteries:** governing body of elders within a local ministry.

{Note: Apostolic Presbyteries *are a counsel {body} of elders that operate in a sent ones {apostolic} anointing that establish, birth, train, send and set other local ministries and leaders teams into the world. Apostolic Presbyteries are NOT limited to these functions, as we will reveal in the following scriptures*}.

{Read: Numbers 27:16-20}

1. Apostolic presbyteries are chosen, sent and set by God. v. 16 { Read: Lk. 6:12-13; Acts 13:1-3; 1 Cor. 12:28; Eph. 2:20}
2. Apostolic presbyteries are governmental for they provide the church with direction and guidance. v. 17, 21
3. Apostolic presbyteries serve as the foundation of the church and also a covering {canopy} for the church and its believers. v. 17 {Read: Eph. 2:20; 4:11; 1 Cor. 12:28}
4. Apostolic presbyteries have the spirit of God dwelling within them. v. 18 {Read: Acts. 3:9}
5. Apostolic presbyteries are confirmed and established through the laying on off hands. v. 18 {Read: Acts 13:1-3}
6. Apostolic presbyteries are given honor and set before the leadership and the people. v. 20
7. Apostolic presbyteries bring the people into a realm of obedience. v. 20
8. Apostolic presbyteries posses the counsel of the Lord. v. 21

{Read: Luke 6:12-13}

1. The members of apostolic presbyteries must have STRONG and CONSISTENT prayer lives. v. 12
   * individual and corporate
2. Apostolic presbyteries are given character and authority by the Lord Jesus Christ. v. 13
   * *whom also he named*: Hebrew word for name is *onoma*, {on-om-ah} which means, a name literally or figuratively; authority, character.

{Read: Acts 13:1-12}

1. Apostolic presbyteries are birthed out of local churches. v. 1
2. Apostolic presbyteries are the government of the local church. v. 1-2 ***Barnabas/Saul**: Apostle , **Lucius**: a teacher, **Simeon** and **Manaen**: Prophets or teachers {*prophetic teacher*}. **Prophetic teachers* are teachers who *prophesy* or Prophets who *teach* {Read: Acts 4:36-37; 11:19-26; 1 Cor. 12:28}
3. Apostolic presbyteries are made up of the APOSTLE, PROPHET, and TEACHER. v. 2{1 Cor. 12:28; Eph. 2:20}* Jesus Christ represents the teacher in Eph. 2:20 {Read: Jn. 3:2}
4. Apostolic presbyteries are birthed through ministering to the Lord, prayer and fasting. v. 2 {Read: Acts 14:23}
5. Apostolic presbyteries carry ministers along with them to train and serve as helpers. v. 50{Read: Acts 13:13}
6. Apostolic presbyteries can be stationary in a local house or travel as teams. v. 4-6
7. Apostolic presbyteries primary enemy is that of the *false prophet* and *witchcraft* that link up with the local spiritual and/or natural government. v. 6-8 * Bar-jesus, *was with Sergius Paulus the deputy of the country*.
8. Apostolic Presbyteries can function as a team or individually. {Acts 13:1-11}
9. Apostolic presbyteries carry the doctrine of deliverance within them. v.12

{Read: Acts 14:23}

1. Apostolic presbyteries suffer much *persecution* to enter, and to bring others into the kingdom of God. v. 19, 22 {Read: Jn. 15:20 Acts 6:5-9; 7:59; 8:2; 11:19; 14:19; 16:16; 2 Tim 3:12} * *Persecute: to harass with unjust punishment; to afflict for adherence to a particular creed. Persecution: act or practice of persecuting; state of being persecuted; continued annoyance.*
2. Apostolic presbyteries carry the anointing of resurrection and healing. v. 20 {Read: Acts 3:1-11}
3. Apostolic presbyteries *confirm* and exhort new converts. v. 22 * Confirm: Greek word is *episterizo* which means; reestablish, to support further and strengthen. {Read: Acts 15:41}
4. Apostolic presbyteries ordain {set in place} other elders. v. 23
5. Apostolic presbyteries establish other presbyteries within regions. v. 23 {Read: Titus 1:5}

{Read: Acts 15:36-41}

1. Apostolic presbyteries revisit ministries they have established. v. 36
2. Apostolic presbyteries must beware of conflicts and splits within their structure. v. 37
3. Apostolic presbyteries must understand everyone on the team will not be able to handle every journey. v. 38 {Ref Acts 13:13}
4. Apostolic presbyteries must be people of *patience, grace, mercy* and *forgiveness*. v. 39 ***Barnabas**: *son of consolation {encouragement}*. {Read: Acts 4:36-37; 2 Cor. 12:12}
5. There is no set leader of apostolic presbyteries Jesus Christ is the HEAD. *LEADERSHIP and MEMBERSHIP may change and shift but HEADSHIP never changes. {Read: Barnabas and Saul; Acts 9:27; 11:25, 30 and then Paul and Barnabas; Acts 13:43}
6. Apostolic presbyteries should be commended and or recommended before they go out. v. 40 {Read: v. 33; 14:26}* Commend: to commit to the care of; to praise. Recommend: To praise to another; to make acceptable, to commit with prayers; to advise. ***Apostolic presbyteries also commend the brethren.** {Read: Acts 14:23; 20:30}
7. Apostolic presbyteries confirm churches. v. 41

{Read: Acts 16:1-24}

1. Apostolic presbyteries go into regions and find believers to train. v. 1-2
2. To be part of any apostolic presbytery, one must have a good report, especially among the brethren. v. 2 {Read: Acts 11:24; 1 Tim. 3:1-2}
3. Apostolic presbyteries have the ability to teach others how to adapt to their surroundings. v. 3 {Read: Acts 21:24-26; 1 Cor. 9:19-23}
4. Apostolic presbyteries are sent through the region to deliver the decrees of local the elders. v. 4.
5. Apostolic presbyteries establish churches in the faith. v. 5
6. Apostolic presbyteries cause the local ministry to increase in faith and number. v. 5 {Read: Acts 2:41; 6:7}
7. Apostolic presbyteries must be sensitive to the leading of the Holy Spirit. v. 6-8
8. Apostolic presbyteries must speak only in the places the Holy Spirit instructs. v. 6-8 {Mat. 10:1-6}
9. Apostolic presbyteries are men and women of vision. v. 9
10. Apostolic presbyteries must be able to connect with the prayers {needs} of the people. v. 9
11. Apostolic presbyteries are able to hear the needs of a region and its people before they even enter into the region. v. 9
12. Apostolic presbyteries not only hear and connect to the needs of the region, they respond. v.10
13. Apostolic presbyteries cannot be lazy, procrastinators, they must move within the timing and seasons of God. v. 10 * *Immediately*
14. Apostolic presbyteries are attracted to the anointing of prayer, for they are birthed from prayer. v. 11
15. Apostolic presbyteries have a heart for women. v. 13 {Read: Jam. 1:27; Phil. 4:3}
16. Apostolic presbyteries have people in each region strategically set up just for them. v. 14-15 {Read: 18:9-10}
17. Apostolic presbyteries baptize in spirit and water. v. 15 {Read: Acts 8:15-17}
18. When apostolic presbyteries enter into a region they stir up demonic activity. v. 16-18

5. **Breast plate of righteousness**. v. 14 {Read: Neh. 4:16; Is. 59:17; Eph. 5:9}
6. **Shoes:** preparation of the *gospel of peace*. v. 15 * In Roman culture their soldiers wore special shoes called *Caligae*. These shoes would allow the solider to advance against his enemy. In this light, the gospel of peace, that is with in the shoe, gives the believer freedom from fear and anxiety as they advance towards their enemy. The believer not only advances in peace but they leave tracks of peace and beauty. {Read: Is. 52:7; Rom. 10:15}
7. **Shield of faith**. v. 16 {Read: 1 Tim. 6:12} The Greek word for *shield* is {thureus-thoo-reh-os} a large shield; a piece of armor worn on the forearm to ward off blows; one that guards, protects, etc. to defend; protect. The Greek word for *faith* is {pistis-pis-tis} persuasion, credence, moral conviction {of religious truth, or the truthfulness of God}, especially reliance upon Christ for salvation; assurance, belief, faith, fidelity. Our shields of faith *quenches* {gk. Sbennumi-sben-noo-mee}, extinguishes and/or puts out the *fiery* {gk. pouroo-poo'-ro-o} ignited, refined, inflamed {with anger, grief, lust} *darts* {gk. Belos-be'-os} missile; spears or arrows.
8. **Helmet of salvation**. v. 17 {Read: Is. 59:17} The bible says we should *take* {gk. Dechomai-dekh-om-ahee} to receive; accept; to get hold of the *helmet* {gk. perikefalaia-per-ee-kef-al-ah'-yah} encirclement of the head. The helmet of salvation when used properly protects the believers from the attacks of doubt {*fiery darts that get pass the shield*} concerning their salvation and assurance of their authority, power and place in regards to the kingdom. {*protects the mind*}
9. **Sword of the Spirit** which is the *word of God*. v. 17 * The sword {word} is kept in our hearts {holster}, and held and or used by our mouth {hand}. {Read: Ps. 119:11; Jer.1:9; Ezek. 2:8; 3:2-3; Rev. 1:16}
10. **Prayer**. v. 18 * *fasting* {Read: Est. 4:16; Mk. 9:29}
11. **Discernment**. v. 18 * *watching* {Read: Ps. 139.2; 2 Pet. 1:9; 2 Cor. 2:1}
12. **Perseverance**. v. 18 *see *stand*

⇒ TYPES OF WEAPONS

* The prophetic words within our spiritual warfare prayers take on the shape of weapons of mass destruction and instruments of death. One must be skillfully in their usage.

1. **Axes** {maces} Maces are upgrades of the club. Having designed metal heads for these clubs they posses a greater force in hand to hand combat. God is definitely calling back the warriors that are skillful with axes. Therefore, we must learn from those who have failed in times past having the heads their axes fall off due to it being made incorrectly and or used improperly. {Read: 2 Kin. 6:5-7; Jer. 51:20}
2. **Battering Rams** {engines of war}. {Read: Ezek. 26.9}
3. **Bow** {quiver} and **Arrows**. {Read: Ps 7:12-13} Our prayers take on the shape of bows that shoot flaming poisonous arrows of the Lord's deliverance. These arrows {prophetic words} smite, poison and consume the enemy. {Read: 2 Kin. 13:17-19}
4. **Brooms** of **destructions**. {Read: Is. 14:23} the Holy Spirit, through the prayer of the believer has the ability to send God's judgment sweeping across the region.
5. **Flaming torches** and **chariots**. {Read: Nah. 2:3-4}* Chariots in biblical times were like our modern day army tanks. These chariots would often have sharp objects attached to their wheels. The speed of the chariot combined with reflection of the sun upon the protruding objects made the chariots look like flaming torches. The light would cause a distraction {temporary blindness} as the chariot cut down all in its path. Our chariot is the Holy spirit, the sharp object would be the word of God. As we move in and by the Holy Spirit {chariot} the light of the SON begins to reflect off our swords {words out of our mouths} causing a distraction to the enemy allowing us to cut down all enemies in our path.
6. **Hoofs** and **Horns**. {Read: Mic. 4:13} * *Break nations to pieces*
7. **Javelin** and **Spears** {*darts, hand pike, hand staff, throwing stick*} {Jos. 8:18-19; 2 Sam. 18:14; Ezek. 39:9}
8. **Mounts.** {Read: Is. 29:3; Jer. 6;6} entrenchment, siege-work, palisade, posts. Mounts are stations of soldiers (garrisons) used to attack the walls of strongholds. Usually these garrisons climb walls by building ramps, ladders and dirt hills to breech the walls of the kingdom desired to over take.
9. **Noise of whips, wheels and horses**. {Read: Nah. 3:2} The power of our prayer produces a sound in the spirit realm of cracking whips, spinning crushing wheels, and charging horses, which causes the enemy to flee or die. {Read: Jud. 7:21-22}
10. **Nose hooks** and **mouth bits**. {Read: Is. 37:29} Our prayer has the ability to control the enemy, literally turning them wherever we direct them.
11. **Red Shields** and **Scarlet garments**. {Read: Nah. 2:3} The primary color of Medo-Babylonian army was red. {Read: Ezek. 23:14} The *red shields* and *scarlet garments* would strike a terror and fear in the heart of the enemy as they approached the cities. As believers, we should have our garments and shields dipped in the BLOOD OF JESUS CHRIST {Read: Rev. 19:13} in doing so, *we strike terror and fear in the heart of the enemy as we approach their territory*. {Read: Acts 5:28}
12. **Shepard's Staff**. {Read: Ex. 4:17;1 Sam.17:40; Ps 23:4} The Shepard's staff comforts, protects, disciplines, guides and produces miracles, signs and wonders.
13. **Sling shots** and **stones**. {Read: 1 Sam. 17:40; 25:29; Jer. 10:18} Stones made of clay or lime stones were fashioned and hurled by shepherds and warriors. Sling shots and stones are most effective from long distances. {Read: Job 41:28; Zech. 9:15}
14. **Sword** and **Daggers**. {Read: Jud. 3:16-22} these mini knives were most effective in hand to hand combat for they can be hidden.
15. **Threshing sledges** with sharp teeth. {Read: Is. 41:15} * Our prayers have the ability to cut down and crush high places.

16. **Trumpets pitchers** and **lamps**. {Read: Judges 7:21} * The sound {trumpets} of our words crashing {pitchers} against the ground {foundations} of the enemy strongholds as we hold our lamps cause the enemy to see and hear an exceedingly great army.
17. **War club**. {Read: Jer. 51:20} *shatters and destroys kingdoms*

⇒ SPIRITUAL WARFARE DEMONSTRATION

There are many forms of prophetic demonstration within intercessory prayer and or spiritual warfare. The leadership of the intercessory and deliverance teams must be open to the Holy Spirit during corporate prayer movements. Leadership must continue to be sober and discerning for false moves that can cause confusion. {Read: 1 Cor. 14:29-33}

1. **Clapping of hands** and **stomping of feet.** {Read: Ezek. 6:11 NIV} Literally drives the devil out of his place. {Read: Job 27:23} Ushers in the judgment and destruction of the Lord. {Ps. 98:8-9; Ezek. 25:6} Exhibits the joy of the Lord. {Read: Is. 55:12; Na. 3:19}manifest a form of mocking, ridicule and delight over another's injury. {Read: Lam. 2:15} Serves as a seal of approval or acceptance. {Read: 2 Kin. 11:12}
2. **Dancing, leaping and running**: Victory, Joy and Happiness. {Read: 2 Sam. 6:14} Praise and Worship {Read: Ps. 149:3; 150:4} Deliverance. {Read: Ps. 30:11} Produces songs and singing in the spirit. {Read: 1 Sa. 21:11; 29:5}
3. **Laughter**. Laughter can break the power of depression and/or oppression. {Read: Neh. 8:10} Laughter also mocks the enemy, while showing the believer that the enemies end is near. {Read: Ps. 37:12-13}
4. **Moaning** and **Groaning**. Grief, Pain and suffering. {Read: Ex. 2:23-24} Intercession. {Read: Rom. 8:26-27}
5. **Shouting** loud. {Read: Josh. 6:16-21; Jer. 51:14} * The shout of the king is in this place {within us}. Num. 23:21, once this shout is released it either does battle against the enemies forces and/or declares a sound of victory.
6. **Tears, Crying** and **Weeping**. {Read: Mal. 2:13} Types of offering and intercession. Tears, Crying and weeping are ways of asking for help or assistance. {Read: Acts 21:28} Prayer and supplication. {Read: Heb. 5:7} Worship
7. **Treading Feet**. {Read: Ps. 44:5; 60:12; 108:13; Lk. 10:19} Tread: To walk on, in or along; to press or beat with the feet, {Serpant: Greek-*ophis*: artful, malicious, a type of sly cunning person. Scorpion: Greek-*skorpios*: to pierce; from its sting}. *As the believer treads with their feet they beat and press he stinging and piercing power of satanic words.* Treading also represents the *fury of the Lord*. {Read: Is. 63:3}

⇒ WEAPONS MAINTENANCE AND UPGRADE

As believers we must not become comfortable with their *weapons performance*. Understanding the importance of **weapons maintenance** and upgrade is very vital. Within battle and war nations constantly competed to develop greater weapons to obtain and edge over their opponent. For example; whenever one nation developed a shield that could not be penetrated by their rivals arrows, their opponent set out to fashion a more powerful and effective arrow. There is a parallel view in the spirit that we must understand, and that is, as we {believers} strengthen, and become more accurate within the usage of our weapons and armor, the enemy sets out to create more weapons that can break through our defenses. So our opening statement must become reality as we further the Kingdom of God. {Read: 1 Sam. 13:21; Ezek. 21:9-11}

RESTORING REGIONS NOTES
CHAPTER 3

Take the time to write down a **power principal** or **teaching** from this chapter of the manual that sticks out to you the most.

_____
_____
_____
_____
_____
_____
_____
_____
_____
_____
_____
_____
_____
_____
_____
_____
_____
_____
_____
_____
_____
_____
_____
_____
_____
_____
_____

Chapter 4: Mapping Regions

BENCHMARKS

A. SCOUTING THE REGION
B. REGIONAL SURVEYING
C. REGIONAL DNA
D. COUNTING THE COSTS
E. REGION RESTRICTION

PROPHETIC EXHORTATION
{Prov. 11:14; 24:6; Heb. 1:1-2}

As we go into new and uncharted regions we must effectively execute the purposes of God. This can only be accomplished if we have taken the necessary precautions to bring God's models {patterns} into fruition. One way of causing God's designs to earth themselves is done through ***spiritual mapping*** of the area {region} we are called to. Whenever God gave and/or gives a command He also provides a strategy on how to accomplish that task. As you continue in this chapter I pray that God begins to unveil your region to you that you might receive His apostolic archetype to invite the habitation of the Lord into your region. Remember every region is not designed the same. Therefore I admonish the reader NOT to limit God or yourself to the techniques within this manual and to seek the Father's counsel.

⇒ A. SCOUTING THE REGION

Mapping: to make a map of or plan. Arrange, layout, set out to do. First when scouting out a region one should have a map of their state and or city along with their governmental structure. Second there should be a plan and or strategy designed to effectively execute the mission.

{Read: Numbers 13: 1-4}

Before a region can be overtaken, we must send scouts {spies} into the land. These scouts should have the ability to discern a people and the land to ensure the proper tactics for regional take over. These agents operate undercover to gather information about the enemy's manpower, defenses, and the lands fertility. {Read: Jos. 2:1; Jud. 18:11-17; Lk. 9:51-52; Acts 19:21; Heb. 11:31; Ja. 2:25} *See section on *scouting teams*.

⇒ B. REGIONAL SURVEYING
{the land and its inhabitants}

{Read: Deuteronomy 7: 1-2}

Upon the entering of a city or battle, one must know what they are up against. There are unseen forces that we must be aware of that will come against {resist} our campaigns. Knowledge is the key to not only our survival but also our advancement {growth}. {Read: Prov. 8:12; 24:6; Hosea 4:6; 2 Pet. 3:18} God gave a clear picture to the children of Israel of what they were going to come up against. For example their were *seven* different nations that the Lord promised He would drive out of the promise land. I believe that each of these nations had specific demonic activity attached to it thus the Lords warning not to mix with them. Here is a list of those nations and what I believe are the forces behind them.

- **Hittites:** {Heb. *Chittiy– khit-tee'*} derived from {Heb. *cheth-khayth*} meaning *terror*, and {Heb. *Chathath -khaw-thar'*} which means to prostrate; hence to break down, either by **violence, confusion** and *fear*:-abolish, affright, be {make} afraid, amaze, beat down, **discourage**, {cause to} dismay, go down, **scare, terrify**. The Hittites were one of the three tribes that inhabited the Palestine and Syria areas.

    ⇒ The *Semites*, nomadic and pastoral tribe.
    ⇒ The *Phoenicians were* merchants and traders.
    ⇒ The *Hittites were the* warriors of the region.

Firmly connected with the Ammorites, they were also known for dwelling in the mountains {high places, pride, haughtiness, and arrogance} {Read: Num. 13:29} This spirit **attacks or lodges** {hides out} **in the mind and or heart.**

- **Girgashities:** Nothing is really known about this particular tribe but that they are **descendants of the fifth son of Canaan** {Read: Gen. 10:16} that dwelt among clayey soil. History also records that they were a branch of a great family of the *Hivites*. It has been told that the Girgashites *might have dealt heavily with the occult. {Spiritism, witchcraft, familiar spirits, etc.}* If at all true, than **these spirits would attack or lodge itself in the mind and rooted in generational curses**.
- **Amorites:** {Heb. *Emoriy– em-o-ree'*} which means *mountaineer*. which represents; *boastfulness, being proud*, pride and/or high places. {mountain dwellers} This spirit **attacks or lodges** {hides out} **in the mind.** {Read: Jos. 10:16}

- **Canaanites:** {Heb. Kenaaniy-ken-ah-an-ee} which means a *peddler*, *merchant*, *trafficker*. The spirit of the merchant is the spirit, I believe, that has infiltrated the body of Christ presently. Jesus Christ, as well as, the Prophet Jeremiah had to combat this same spirit which is linked to *pride, high-mindedness, greed, lust for riches, power, prosperity, money, wealth, filthy lucre*. {Read: Jer. 7:11; Mat. 21:12-13; 1 Tim. 6:17} The Canaanites were the birthing place of the other tribes {Jebusites, Amorites, and the Girgashites}. The Canaanites dwelt by the sea. {Read: Num. 13:29} Water is symbolic of the spirit and word of God. {Read: Jn. 3:5; 6:63; Eph. 5:26} **This spirit attacks or lodges** {hides out} **in the spirit and/or words of the believer**. Also can be found **in the heart** and **mind** as well.

- **Perizzites:** {*Heb. Perizziy-per-iz-zee*} meaning *inhabitants of the open country*. Another word for {*Heb. Perowzi-per-o-zee*} which means *a rustic person. Rustic*: the country, rural, simple or artless, rough or uncouth, a country person. {country bumpkin} One of the nations that was conquered by Joshua {Read: Jos. 24:11} but still allowed to dwell in the land as servants through the administration of Solomon. {Read: 1 Kin. 9:20} **This spirit targets or lodges** {hides out} **in the mind, heart and character** {soul}. Also represents the things {sins} that we conquer {get control over} but don't do away with, then have serve us. {ie. The person stops fornicating but keeps the boyfriend or girlfriend around to gain, money, clothes, bill payment, and/or companionship {for those that fear being alone} It has also been said that this nation was also known for *prostitution, deception* and *seduction*.

- **Hivites:** {Heb. Chivviy-khiv-vee} which means a villager. Were known as "midlanders" or "villagers". The prince of the Hivites was *Hamor* {Read: Gen. 24:2-28} who's name meant "donkey" Donkeys, as we all know, are very *headstrong* {stubborn} and *untamed*. {Read: Hos. 8:9}. Donkeys were used to trample seeds, to turn the millstone to grind grain and pull plows. Donkeys were also used as modes of transportation. So it would be safe to say that the ruling sprit over this nation could have been *stubbornness, stiff-necked,* and *hardness of heart even slothfulness, pride* and *even vanity*. just to name a few. **This spirit targets or lodges** {hides out} **in the heart, neck, back and/or legs** to keep the people from moving forward. It can also **lodge in the mindset of the people** to keep them from moving into new revelations of the Lord or hearing and/or responding to the commandments of God. Once this "donkey spirit" or donkey people are TAMED and in motion they can carry twice its weight in load and work very hard, which reveals another spirit of *double-mindedness*. {sometimes working hard, some times hardly working} King Solomon also allowed this spirit to stay in his land as well. {Read: 1 Kin. 9:20}

- **Jebusites:** {Heb. Yebuwc-yeb-oos} The Jebusites were defeated by Joshua {Read: Jos. 10:16-27} but were not driven out of Jebus {Jerusalem} The Jebusites claimed rule over the city called Jebus {Jerusalem} which later became controlled by King David and renamed "*City of David*" the capital of David's kingdom. **The spirits hides out in the caves of the mind, body and soul, that formulate strongholds.**

{Read: Ephesians 6:12}

- **Principalities:** {Gk. Arche} a commencement or chief. principle, rule, beginners, corner, first, magistrate, power, applications of order, time, place or rank. A powerful ruler, or the rule of someone in authority. The word principalities {often in the plural} may refer to human rulers. {Read: Titus 3:1} Any type of rule other than God Himself.

  * There are three types of principalities.
  - ⇒ Human Principalities {Read: Titus 3:1}
  - ⇒ Demonic Principalities {Read: Dan. 10:13, 20; Rom. 8:38; Eph. 6:12; Col. 2:15}
  - ⇒ Angelic Principalities {Read: 1 Cor. 11:10; Rom. 8:38; Eph. 3:10; Col. 1:16}

- **Powers:** {Gk. Exousia} Mastery, magistrate, superhuman potentate, token of control, delegate, influence, authority, jurisdiction. {Read: Eph. 3:10; Lk. 12:11; Rom. 13:1; Col. 1:16; Ti. 3:1}

- **Rulers of Darkness: Rulers:** {Gk. kosmokrator} comes from {gk. Kosmos– orderly arrangement decoration, world. A world ruler. An epithet of Satan. {epithet-any word implying a quality attached to a person or thing. Ruler of Darkness is a Ruler or leader that BELONGS TO darkness.

Darkness: {Gk. Skotos} shadiness, obscurity. The absence of light. {Read: Gen. 1:2} Associated with chaos, evil, bad luck, affliction, death {Job 7:12; 21:17; 10:21-22; 38:17} ignorance and sin. {Job 24:13-17}

Rulers of darkness can also be linked to **ruler of the synagogue.**

- ⇒ *Jairus:* {Read: Mk. 5:22; Lk. 8:41}
- ⇒ *Crispus:* {Read: Acts 18:8}
- ⇒ *Sosthenes:* {Read: Acts 18:17}

- ♦ **Spiritual Wickedness:**

  Spiritual: {Gk. *Pneumatikos*} {humanly} ethereal a spirit or supernatural, regenerate, religious. *Ethereal:* of or relating to the regions beyond the earth celestial, heavenly, unworldly and spiritual
  Wickedness: {Gk. *Poneria*} depravity {making bad or worse, to impair the good qualities, to corrupt, to violate} malice {a disposition to injure others, spite, ill-will, rancor} {Read: Rom. 1:29-32}

{Read: Colossians 1:16}

- ♦ **Thrones:** {Gk. Thronos} a stately seat, a potentate, power. The chair of a king, throne in a symbol of royal government. A royal power and dignity, sovereignty, **an order of angels**. Can refer to a king's role as judge. {Read: Ps. 122:5; Is. 16:5; acts; 7:49; Col. 1:16; Rev. 3:21; 4:2}
- ♦ **Dominions:** {Gk. *Kuriotes*} **an order of angels,** mastery, rulers, government. Sovereign authority, district, governed, reign, absolute ownership. {Read: Eph. 1:21; Col. 1:16}
- ♦ **Virtues**: "might", "Virtues" or "Strongholds" {Gk word for "might" is dynamies which translates into virtues} **An order of angels**. These mighty ones lay beyond the *ophanim* (Thrones/Wheels). Their primary duty is to supervise the movements of the heavenly bodies in order to ensure that the cosmos remains in order. {Read: Eph. 1:21)

⇒ C. REGIONAL DNA

DNA is the basic chromosome material {genes}, containing and transmitting the hereditary pattern. Therefore regional DNA deals with the *make up* of the city, region, etc. In order to determine this, one must research the history of the place they are sent to. Each city, just as a person, has spiritual chromosomes {DNA} that contains and transmits hereditary patterns. Just as the DNA of the person can be altered, the DNA of any given city can be altered as well. **Regional Restoration** is bringing the land and its people back to its divine order {pattern} that was set by God {Read: Gen. 1:26-28} and that was altered by Satan. {Read: Gen. 3:1-19} I believe the DNA of a region can be detected by uncovering the **spiritual climate**, **attitude** and **state** of the area.

Here is an example on how to detect spiritual DNA of a region. We will use the history of Crete to unveil the spiritual DNA of this region.

- ♦ Crete was the city Paul sent one of his sons {Titus} to establish order and raise more leaders within the city. {Titus 1:5}
- ♦ Crete is an island that is located in the Mediterranean Sea, which made the region subject to all sorts of storms. Paul experienced the first part of the cities DNA first hand, when his ship was struck by a storm call *Euroclydon*, which means *strong, violent wind*. {Acts 27:7-8 12-14, 21} which shows the...

  Spiritual Climate: Strong, Violent {hostile}

- ♦ Crete is also identified with Caphtor the place of origin of the Philistines {Gen. 10:14; Deut. 2:23; Amos 9:7} Also home of the Cherethites {Ezek. 25:16} who had association with the Philistines. Philistines are the ones who constantly fought against God and His people. {Jud. 14-18; 1 Sam. 10:5} {Philistines comes from a *gk* word meaning, roll {in the dust} roll {wallow} self.
- ♦ Cretian legend says that Crete was governed {ruled} by King Minos and the Minotaur {a half-bull, half-man monster} which shows the...

(Continued from page 90)

Spiritual Attitude: Prideful and Rebellious
- Crete was captured by the Romans in 68-66 B. C. and made a Roman Province. History tells us that whenever a land or people is taken over by another, that particular region is made to take on the practices, laws, customs, etc. of the conquering foe. {Deut. 7:1-4} This tells us the...

Spiritual State: Bound/Captive

The spiritual DNA or chromosomes that were transmitted were **strong violence, pride**, **rebellion** and **slavery** {being bound/captive}. Though the Cretians had an encounter with God's power at the day of Pentecost, {Acts 2:1-11} the regions DNA, through time, slowly transformed the people into *liars, evil beasts,* and *slow bellies*. {Titus 1:12} So as believer we must understand that as we do great exploits for the Jesus Christ we not only have to fight the inhabitants {devils} of the land but we must be prepared to fight against the land itself

⇒ D. COUNTING THE COSTS

{Read: Num. 13:18-20 Luke 14:28-33}

Every area must be must be assessed, no rock can be left unturned. Every I must be dotted and every T must be crossed. There can be no room left for miscalculations or error. This should be mindset of the regional teams as they go forth in their quests for God. All supplies, finances, troops etc. should be accounted for. Any miscalculations can cause the teams devastating, as well as, long term effects. Counting the cost not only deals with what we should have before the battle, but also the loss we will suffer because of the battle. {Josh. 7:1-5; Is. 8:15; Jn. 6:66; 2 Thes. 2:3; 1 Tim. 4:1; 1 Pet. 4:18}

⇒ E. REGION RESTRICTIONS.

{Read: Romans 15:18-21}

1. Our words can sometimes be restricted according to the regions they are released in. v. 18 {Read: Acts 16:6-7}
2. Our regions will only respond to the voices that are within legally ordained limits. v.18 {Read: 2 Cor. 10:13-16}
3. In our efforts to restore regions we mustn't over step our boundaries. v. 18
4. There are spiritual land marks and boundary lines {property lines} throughout the lands and we must be cognizant of them and not cross or remove them unless instructed by God. v. 19 {Read: Gen. 10:19; 31:43-53; Deut. 19:14; Ps. 19:4; Hos. 5:10}
5. Building on another man's property can cause God's KINGDOM to be built upward and not spread out. v.20 {Read: 1 Cor. 3:10-17} * BUILDINGS go up but KINGDOMS spread out.

In conclusion of this chapter, I would like share one more important insight. Though your area may have more than one ministry, church, etc within it, it DOES NOT mean that the name of Jesus Christ is being or has been preached. For example; more than 1 ministry per block or more than 7 in an area, one must assess the neighborhood, community and its people before counting that area out for building. For if the TRUE JESUS CHRIST is being administered CHANGE should occur in the area. If change is not happening then it is safe to say that JESUS CHRIST has not been preached or truly demonstrated. {Read: Rom. 8:20} Useful resources of regional growth can be obtained at **local police departments, word of mouth** {residents} and **regional statistics via the internet**.

RESTORING REGIONS NOTES
CHAPTER 4

Take the time to write down a **power principal** or **teaching** from this chapter of the manual that sticks out to you the most.

Chapter 5: Entering A Region

BENCHMARKS

I. LEARNING THE LANGUAGE
II. TRAVEL & ESCAPE ROUTES
III. TRAVELING UNANNOUNCED
IV. SET UP SAFE HOUSES
V. HEADQUARTER & FIELD UNITS

PROPHETIC EXHORTATION
{Mat. 10:1-15}

Now as you embark upon the next phase of your life, I pray that all that have heard the call answered, and embraced their charges. I decree that everything your teams have ascertained will be remembered and utilized. Possess the gates of the enemy, for you are part of a mighty army that cannot be stopped. I release spiritual discernment and focus. I pray that you and your teams obtain help from the sanctuary and strength from out of Zion. I pray that your tracks be covered under the blood of Jesus Christ, and the plans, schemes and traps of the enemy be uncovered. Strength and power to the posts of your tents and barracks. May the foundations of your command posts run deep and stand the test of time. I pray that your flight be not in winter.

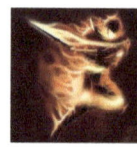

ENTERING THE REGION

Enter: To come or go into; to penetrate; to insert, to become a member of or participant. To get a person admitted.

I. LEARNING THE LANGUAGE

In order to enter a region you must know and understand their language. Every region has a gate keeper. The gatekeeper responds to the secret codes {languages} of that particular region and or people. All those that have these codes are allowed entrance into the region. If we do not produce the correct sound, gesture, movement, etc. that they are accustomed to then we will be denied entrance. It's very important that we know the verbiage of the regions inhabitants that we may understand secret plans that might be distributed. {Read: 1 Kin. 18:26-28} For example, most gangs, fraternities and high society clubs have secret handshakes, passwords, etc. that allows there members access to the group. We must be bilingual in the spirit and not ignorant concerning any of the devils devices. As we learn the languages of our regions we gain control of the gates, allowing the Spirit of God and His armies entrance. {Read: Gen. 22:17; Judges 12:5-6; Acts 2: 4-11; 21:36-40; 22:1-7; 1 Cor. 9:20-22; 13:1; 2 Cor. 2:11}

II. ESTABLISHING TRAVEL AND ESCAPE ROUTES

Before a team can effectively enter into the region they must establish travel and escape routes. Travel routes allow swift and safe passage through the region. {Read: Jud. 8:11; Jn. 7:1} Escape routes are to be set in case there is a strong attack not calculated. When this occurs and a team must abort the mission until a later time. The escape route permits the team to exit quickly and safely. {Read: Josh. 2:16, 22-23; Mat. 10:16}

III. COMING AND GOING UNANNOUNCED

Teams must be sure they bring no attention to themselves. {Read: Jos. 2:1; Phil. 2:7-8} Being noticed can be detrimental to a mission. {Read: Mt. 8:4; 16:20; Mk. 1:24} Exposure can result in capture, possible death, which will undoubtedly bring set back to the mission. {Read: Jn. 7:1-8} *See counting the costs.*

IV. SET UP SAFE HOUSES

Every team must set up place in the region that they can use as a safe house. {Read: Jos. 2:1} These safe houses are usually viewed as places to do stake outs or hideouts. Rest, shelter, food, etc. are usually found in these places. *Find places in the neighborhood, community, city around the area your team is called to and set up a relationship with the owners of that place. Allow the Holy Spirit to lead the team to the place. Reveal to the safe house owner your mission and they will help. Each city region has safe houses strategically set up for teams.* {Read: Acts 16:14-15; 18:9-10} Keep in mind not all safe houses know that this is what they are. Also remember that not every helper in the city {region} will be a saint {saved}.

⇒ V. ESTABLISHING HEADQUARTERS

Headquarters: Headquarters is where all team members report and bring all information received through their surveillance of the land. **Headquarters** is also where teams are birthed, stationed, sometimes temporarily, trained, equipped and sent out. **Headquarters** should be the central location of your operation {base}. Headquarters {command posts} are usually set up in the vicinity of the area the team wants to patrol, govern, and or subdue. Notice in *Numbers 13:1-3* the children of Israel were stationed *outside* of Canaan.

Spies were sent *from* the wilderness of Paran {v. 3} to spy out Canaan. Using this pattern gives a team a better view of the territory it has been sent to take over. This brings to mind an old saying "We can see more on the OUTSIDE looking IN."

I believe the New Testament Church followed these same patterns.

The Church **AT** Antioch, {Acts 13:1}
The Church **OF** Ephesus and the Laodiceans {Rev. 2:1; 3:14}
The Church **IN** Smyrna, Pergamos, Thyatira, Sardis and Philadelphia {Read: Rev. 2:8, 12, 18; 3:1, 7}

AT denotes: near by, to or toward.
OF denotes: coming from, resulting from, made from, or belonging to.
IN denotes: living or located in.

God was addressing His church {troops} made up of ALL believers stationed in, around, or belonging to those geographical locations, mentioned giving them words of encouragement, correction, and instruction. Therefore, being out of the correct position, we could endanger ourselves as well as others. When the CHIEF commander {God }comes looking for US as the NOW Testament church} will we be found in the place were He sent or set us? {Read: Gen.3:9} *Headquarter* positioning plays a vital part of our mission being fulfilled effectively.

⇒ F. SETTING UP FIELD UNITS

Once the Headquarters has completed the task of infiltrating the region the **field units** are set in place to assist in the up keep of the territory, I like to call these units **ZONE CONTROL or A.C. UNITS**. *Antioch Churches {Read: Acts 13:1-5}

Field Units {Cell Groups}

Field units are stations that are set up in the *north south east* and *west* sectors of the region. These units are ran by the five-fold ministry. {Read: Ps. 68:18; Acts 13:1-2; 1 Cor. 12:28; Eph. 4:8, 11) The field units objective is to infiltrate the region, sections at a time, giving God and His troops, deeper penetration into the land as they gain more ground. {kingdom advancement}

- **Apostles, Prophet and Teacher:** serve as the government of the field unit {AC Unit} Establishing order and structure to the field unit. Without the proper set government, what I like to call **A. P. T.**, *miracles, healings, helps, governments* and *diverse tongues* will not manifest properly. {Read: 1 Cor. 12:28} Once a unit {local ministry} is set, they usually *wait, work, watch* and *pray* until they receive more instructions from the command post to start another field unit. {**Govern, Guide, Ground**}
- **Pastors:** serve as the keeper {protector & preserver} of the grounds and troops. **Pastors** are positioned **WITHIN** the troops and A. C. Unit to distribute and enforce the commands of the field unit government. {**Guard**} {Read: 1 Pet. 5:1-5}
- **Evangelists:** serve as a type of *reconnaissance specialists*. Instead of collecting information, they collect {enlist} troops {souls}. **Evangelist** rarely take part in running a field unit, **they run FOR the unit**. Evangelists are the church {field units} in motion, they are the ones used to release the fresh, cool air sent from the A.C. Unit in the form of the gospel into the parched regions. Evangelists are sent to bring miracles, deliverance great joy into the city. {**Gather**} {Read: Acts 8:8} * *see scouting teams and evangelism teams.*

We must beware of double agents posing as field units. The units that produce members that are playing on both sides of field. {Read: Ps. 68:18; 2 Cor. 11:12-15} The following diagrams will give you a closer view of what transpires between the headquarters and its field units during regional restoration.

- Headquarters receive instructions from the Chief Commander {God} saying send deliverance into the region {land}. Then headquarters distributes these instructions to the *field units*, located N. E. W. S. of the said region. **{Diagram A}**

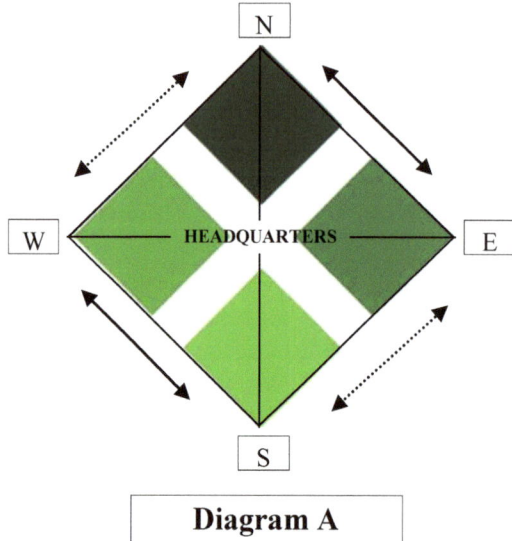

Diagram A

- The **A.C. Units** then put the commands into action. As each field unit administers deliverance in there own areas {N. E. W. S} according to their own graces {gifts & talents} and locations as a unified body, it will cause a shifting in the spirit realm. {paradigm shift}

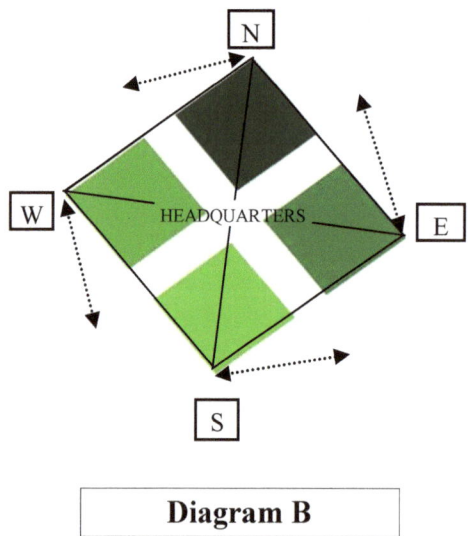

Diagram B

- As the shift continues the region begins to turn like a wheel, creating a unified movement which will produce a whirlwind of deliverance to be released and received from God. Once this takes place the spiritual DNA of the region will change and regional restoration takes place. This corporate move will not only cause the *visitation* of the Lord, but His *habitation which is the desire of the Lord*. {Read: Ex. 15:2; 2 Chr. 6:2}

(Continued from page 97)

RESTORING REGIONS NOTES
CHAPTER 5

Take the time to write down a **power principal** or **teaching** from this chapter of the manual that sticks out to you the most.

Chapter 6
Attacking Your Region

BENCHMARKS

A. BREAKING THE REGION OPEN
   ⇒ AIR ASSAULT

B. INVADING THE REGION
   ⇒ GROUND ASSAULT

PROPHETIC EXHORTATION
{Ezek. 9:1-11}

Attacking the region is one of the most dangerous, yet thrilling parts of your mission. Understanding, knowledge, wisdom and the fruit of Spirit must be allowed to have credence in your total man {body, soul, and spirit}. Along with the fruit of the spirit you must possess a holy indignation inside that will cause the rivers of boldness to flow as you combat the forces of darkness. Stir up those wells of love and compassion inside of you, let them come forth. Fear, doubt, faintheartedness, can have no place beyond this page. All a-wol spirits are bound. I decree that you are ready for this fight. Let nothing separate you or your team from the ultimate goal, total domination and regional restoration. Can you hear the noise of battle, smell the stench of blood, taste the sweet nectar of victory. As enter battle there is no need to be afraid. God did not give you the spirit of fear, but of love peace and a sound mind. I prophesy accuracy to your arrows and sword. Strength to your body and God's divine wisdom on the battle field and planning room. As the clatter of shields, swords and battering rams echo through the land, I declare peace to your spirit and mind. Be strong and very courageous. Remember the Lord is with you there is no need to fear.

⇒ A. BREAKING OPEN THE REGION

Attacking: to set upon or work against forcefully; to assail with unfriendly or bitter words; to begin to affect or to act on injuriously; to set to work on; to threaten (a piece in chess) with immediate capture.

Breaking the region open deals with two fazes which are: *air assault* and *ground* assaults;

⇒ PRAYER & FASTING
⇒ PRAISE & WORSHIP

Depending on the severity of bondage in the area will depict which, will come first. Keep in mind our position in the battle plays an important role as well. If on the *defense* the air attack can sometimes go forth first. When on the *offense* the ground assault may be released first.

1st wave of attack

The first phase deals with *prayer* and *fasting*. As you pray your words serve as flaming arrows, sling shots and catapults with sharp and heavy stones in the spirit, that come down upon the heads of the forces of evil. *Fasting* conditions our natural and spiritual body to endure the long tedious battles. * See section on *spiritual warfare demonstration and team weapons*.

Prayer should include the following. {but not limited to}

- **Repentance:** renouncing and asking for forgiveness for the sins of the land {area} and the inhabitants. Naming the known sins of the area and interceding for the people of the area will give you great leeway. Pray that Godly sorrow and conviction would fill the hearts of men that wide spread repentance might sweep the area. {Read: Jonah 3:5-10} This tactic will also thwart pending judgment. {Read: 1 Sam. 7:3-12; 2 Chr. 7:14} * *see intercessory teams*.
- **Unity:** Pray against and root out the seeds of division, envy, strife and competition and loose destruction upon their works in the area. Pray that God would release oneness in the midst of area leaders and give them a hunger and thirst to unite and become one. {Read: Jer. 1:10; 1 Jn. 3:8; Jn. 17:11; 1 Cor. 1:10; Acts 2:1, 44-46}
- **Vision:** Pray that God will do away with mans visions and that the area leadership will take on His vision for that region. {Read: Hab. 2:2-3}
- **Guidance:** Pray that God would lead and guide His people into the paths of holiness, righteousness and the ways that attract His presence. {Read: Ps. 78:72; Jn. 16:13}
- **Growth:** Pray for the spiritual and natural growth of the true ministries in the area. {Read: Acts 16:4-5}

As *repentance, unity, vision* and *growth* become a part of your daily life of prayer, also compile a list of the demonic forces ruling in your area. This list usually can be obtained from your *scouting teams*. Remember your ministry does not have to be large to exercise these principals. Using local newspapers, word of mouth, your local news and most importantly the HOLY SPIRIT can provide you with a list that can do some tremendous damage if followed.

Once your list is formulated begin to go forth into the mode of **S**trategic **W**arfare **A**nd **T**argeted prayer. I call this mode **S. W. A. T.** If you have to read from the list DO NOT hesitate, there is no rule that says you must pray with our eyes closed. You want to hit the mark and not fight as one beating the air. {Read: 1 Cor. 9:26}

Fasting:
Along with prayer you should have a regular schedule of fasting. {Read: Acts 13:1-2} Fasting is instituted into the believers life to help crucify the flesh. As our flesh dies our spirit lives and grows stronger. Fasting is a part of intercession. Intercession effects your life but it is mainly for the benefit of others. {Read: Ezek. 22:30} Therefore if we do any of these things for the sake of our own name gaining glory, the fruit thereof will be little to none or will grow and not remain at all. {Read: Jn.15:16} Certain generational and area strongholds {curses} cannot be broken with out fasting. {Read: Mat 17:21} this is why Paul admonishes us to give ourselves over to prayer and fasting. {Read: 1 Cor. 7:5}

2nd wave of attack

Praise and **Worship:** is a powerful force, **the second wave to your air attack**. Being a psalmist myself this segment of battle literally makes my hurt burn. King David understood the power and purpose of *praise* and *worship* and how they literally touched the heart of God causing Him to respond. {Read: Ps. 22:3}

As King David moved the ark of the covenant from TENT, to the HOUSE of Obed-edom, INTO the CITY of David {Read: 2 Sam. 6:13}, David himself entered the city with dancing, shouting and music {v. 16}, making alive Psalms 100:4 *enter his gates with thanksgiving and his courts with praise*.

- Praise and Worship is the battering ram that brakes through the spiritual gates of the city, giving entrance to the presence of the Lord.

This prophetic act of love revealed not only the heart David had for God, but for his city.

- Praise and worship reveals the heart of the people and their leaders within their region.
- Praise and worship releases a passion within the land for God's presence.

Just when you think it couldn't get any better. David still wasn't satisfied. A visitation was good but habitation all the more better. David wanted to bring joy to the Lord and not just God's spirit to his city. I believe David appreciated God's presence being with his CITY so much that he didn't want to take any chances on messing that up. So David learned how to entertain the spirit of God to make Him comfortable and His time in the city worth wild, making it hard for the Holy Spirit to leave.

- Praise and Worship cause the Lord to dwell among us.
- Praise and Worship brings pleasure to the Lord and makes our regions irresistible. The devil hates anything that gives God pleasure, for he knows the JOY OF THE LORD is our strength. {Read: Neh. 8:10} When we make God happy, He in turn gives us strength.
- Praise and Worship releases strength and the beauty of God into region. {Read: 2 Chr. 20:21}

Implementing a plan, that I believe was directly from God, David took twenty four groups of twelve and established the first and only 24 hr. praise and worship experience. This band of worshipping warriors became the very foundation and backbone of the Tabernacle of David. {Read: 1 Chr. 25:9-31; Amos 9:11-12; Acts 15:15-17} David also had 4,000 people praising and worshipping God simultaneously. {Read: 1Chr. 23:5} David established a continuous onslaught against Satan's kingdom, while at the same time, making His city conducive for the presence of God to inhabit. {Read: 1 Chr. 16}

- Praise and Worship kick and keeps the devil out, while inviting and keeping the presence of God in.

⇒ B. INVADING THE REGION

Invading the region deals with your *third wave of attack* which is the final faze. Here is the time in battle where you will experience hand to hand combat, up-close and personal.

Third wave of attack {ground assault}

♦ DELIVERANCE & EVANGELISM

Evangelism and **Deliverance** teams are sent out into battle and work closely with the air assault teams. Once the air assault has received the word {instructions from God} to cease firing {Read: Acts 13:1-2; 27:33-37; 1 Cor. 7:5} and to send in the ground troops, then the region is rushed with an onslaught of the word of God {evangelism} and casting out of devils {deliverance}, signs, wonders, miracles, healings, mighty acts and deeds {Read: Acts 6:7-8; 8:4}. As the evangelism and deliverance teams go into battle as God's ambassadors, house to house, throughout neighborhoods and communities the air assault must keep a watchful eye and a discerning spirit. The air assault should be on going as the ground assault advances. {Read: Mat. 28:19-20; Mk. 16:15; Acts 5:42; 2 Cor. 5:18-20} The ongoing air assault becomes the wedge in the spirit to keep your region open for new moves {instructions} of God. {Read: Lk. 18:1; Acts 12:5, 12; 1 Thes. 5:17}

In closing **remember every team should have a strategy**. {Read: Jud. 7:16-25} Also realize that not all strategies work, for they may differ depending on the region. {Read: Jos. 7:1-5} I must put strong emphasis on being LEAD OF THE HOLY SPIIRT. We cannot take the principles, techniques and strategies that are used in one region and try to apply it to another. For example, one cannot build a house in California the same way as he or she would build in Philadelphia. Differences in cost, terrain, weather, etc. One must do much more research when it comes to the building process. This too is a parallel truth for region restoration. You must seek God for the strategy for your region to properly capture it for the Lord.

RESTORING REGIONS NOTES
CHAPTER 6

Take the time to write down a **power principal** or **teaching** from this chapter of the manual that sticks out to you the most.

BENCHMARKS

A. **HARVEST THE REGION**
   ⇒ GATHERING THE SPOILS
   ⇒ DISTRIBUTING THE SPOILS

B. **ESTABLISH THE REGION**
   ⇒ HEALING THE REGION:

C. **PROTECT THE REGION:**
   ⇒ SAFEGUARDING THE REGION
   ⇒ IMPLEMENTING DEFENSE SYSTEMS
   ⇒ REGIONAL TRAFFIC CONTROL

PROPHETIC EXHORTATION
{Is. 40:2-3; 1:19; 2 Tim. 4:7; Mat. 25:21}

Zion I speak to you this day the words of the prophet Isaiah your warfare is accomplished, your regions iniquities have been pardon for you have received double of the Lords hands for your sins. Now eat the good of the land for your willingness and obedience. You have ran the course, fought the fight and kept the faith. Well done my good and faithful servants. Enter into the joy of the Lord.

⇒ HARVEST THE REGION:

Harvest: The gathering in of a crop; the outcome of any effort; to gather.

Gathering the spoils:

After a strong campaign is complete there is nothing left to do but reap the fruit of your labor. A few things must be remembered upon gathering the spoils of victory.

- The spoils are not only souls, but whatever the region has to offer. {Read: Num. 14:21; Ps. 115:16; Is. 1:19}
- The spoils of victory belong to us. {Read: Gen. 14:11-12; 1 Sam. 17:53; Acts 13:19}
- You don't have to fight a war to obtain spoils. {Read: 2 Kin. 7:3-8; Jer. 49:31-32}
- Only take what God says take. {Read: Jos. 6:17-18; Na. 2:9; 2 Cor. 6:17; Col. 2:20-22}
- Give God what belongs to Him. {Read: Mal. 3:7-10}

Distributing the spoils:

To keep the release of the Lord's blessings continuously {Read: Ps. 68:19} flowing in our region we must SHARE the abundance. Every one must possess and equal amount of the spoils that none go lacking. For example; say if when harvesting souls, 50 people come to know the Lord in the region your team campaigns in, Refrain from directing all the people to your ministry {field unit}, find other God *sent-set* ministries that need assistance and refer them to that ministry. Also if you already have an established ministry, say with 200 disciples {members}, send some of them to labor in a vineyard who has less, this will produce growth in the ministries faith, finances and fellowship causing His kingdom to enlarge and our display of love will project to a doubting world and the crippled "church" that God is real and we are His. {Read: Jn. 13:35} The Apostles constantly put this practice into action {Read: Acts 2:41-47; 4:32-37} The reason why a lot of our regions are filled with so much *death* and *poverty* is because no one wants to share {give}.

Everything is kept to themselves, MY ministry, MY people, My gifts, My revelation. Sounds like a Johnny Gill spirit to me. {MY, MY, MY} {Read: Zech. 7:4-7} The entire ministry of Jesus Christ was founded upon principle of giving. He GAVE sight to the blind, He GAVE hearing to the deaf, He GAVE a voice to the dumb, He GAVE the lame the ability to walk, He GAVE healing to the sick, and He GAVE His LIFE for us. For God so love, He GAVE. Need I say more. Giving is the heart of the Father and each time we give with willing hearts we echo the beat of His heart and its rhythm throughout the earth for others to hear and follow. One missionary told me that; *"giving is not a money problem, it's a heart problem"*. {Read: Acts 5:1-10}

- Sharing {giving} breaks the power of poverty and death. {Read: Est. 9:19; Prov. 23:21; Acts 5:1-10}
- The correct distribution of spoils to God and His people releases prosperity into the region. {Read: Mal. 3:10}

B. REESTABLISH THE REGION:

Establish: To order, ordain or enact {a law, etc.}; to set up {a nation, business, etc.}; to cause to be; bring about; to cause to be excepted; to prove; demonstrate; to make firm or stable; to introduce and cause to grow and multiply to bring into existence; to put on a firm basis; to put into a favorable position; to gain full recognition or acceptance of; to make (a church) a national or state institution; to put beyond doubt.

Healing the region:

As we all know that after every war {battle} the land suffers loss as well as gain. This becomes the opportune time for healing to occur. The region has open wounds from battle so the Lord begins to usher in His healing winds and rains of **prophesy** to repair and restore the land. {Read: Is. 58:12; Ezek. 37:1-10; Joel 2:23-28} This **prophetic weather** unleashes strength, settlement, wholeness and life back into your area. {Read: Ezek. 37:1-10; 1 Pet. 5:10}

C. PROTECT THE REGION:

Protect: to **cover** or **shield** from exposure, injury, or destruction; **guard**; to **maintain** the status or integrity of especially through financial or legal guarantees; to **save** from contingent financial loss; to **foster** or shield from infringement or restriction; to **restrict** competition for (as domestic industries) by means of tariffs or trade controls; defend.

Implementing defense systems:

The battle is over, the region has been restored to its divine order, and peace and serenity has entered back into the land, but for how long? Just when you thought it was safe to get back in the swing of things, a greater enemy returns. Now an even worse enemy is upon your regions door step trying to *steal, kill* and *destroy*. But thanks be unto God that causes us to triumph. How so? Two words, DEFENSE SYSTEM. God in His infinite wisdom knows the plans of the devil and reveals them to His people {Read: 2 Cor. 2:11}.

The Father knows that its just a matter of time before the enemy regains his strength, and rallies his forces to come stronger, faster and harder {Read: Gen. 19:9; Hab. 2:1-8; Mat. 12:43-45; Jn. 5:14} Knowing this we must implement a *defense system* that we might be prepared for future attacks. {Read: Nah.2:1} This system CANNOT be ran and or governed by people with a mindset of *fear* or *paranoia*, quick draw McGraws and trigger happy saints are not allowed. {Read: Mk. 14:47; Lk. 9:54} The *defense team* should be sober, alert, prayerful and discerning. Defense teams should be people gifted with far sight, hindsight and insight in the realms of the spirit.

The four lines of defense should consist of:

- **A company of prophets**. Prophets are graced with an in depth view in the spirit realm that no other *gift* of the five-fold {field unit} ministry posses. Amos 3:7 says...*Surely the Lord God will do nothing, but he revealeth his secret unto his servants the **prophets***. {emphasis added} God gives the prophets and or prophetess that are on their posts prophetic insight into pending danger and all the demonic plans of the enemy. {Read: 2 Ki. 6:8-19; Act 11:28; 21:10-11}
- **Apostolic Confederacies** Are networks of cell ministries or churches that come together to defend and fight for the region and its people against a common threat. {Read: Gen. 14:13}
- **Prophetic Garrisons** intercessory and prophetic ministry teams set to guard, protect, either to prevent hostile invasion, or to keep the inhabitants of a besieged city {region} from flight. {Read: 2 Cor. 11:32}

- **Angels**. Angels play a crucial part in the battle for your region. Angels not only provide messages from the Lord, but also offer a wall of protection that cannot be penetrated. {Read: 2 Kin. 6:16-17; Ps. 34:7} Jesus Christ also understood the power and importance of angelic assistance. In Mat. 26:53 Christ's declaration concerning angels is one of the most profound statements in regards to angels.

Thinkest thou that I cannot now pray to my father and he shall presently give me more than twelve legions of angels.

What makes this comment awesome is the history of the word *legion*. Legion is a large group of soldiers; army; a large number; a multitude. In Roman culture a roman legion consisted of 6,000 men. For the math buffs, 12 x 6000 = 72,000. Christ is saying I can pray to the Father and He would send MORE THAN twelve legions or MORE THAN 72,000 angels to His aide. Now according to Is. 37:36 just one angel alone can defeat 185,000 men just imagine what damage 72,000 angels can do. My God, angelic defense is truly a source of protection that no one can deny and would be absolutely foolish not to utilize. Angels are released, set in place and or activated by words. {Read: Ps. 103:20-21; Dan. 3:16-18, 24-28; 6:16, 21-22; 10:12} * *God's words out of our mouth.*

RESTORING REGIONS NOTES
CHAPTER 7

Take the time to write down a **power principal** or **teaching** from this chapter of the manual that sticks out to you the most.

PROPHETIC EXHORTATION
{1 Jn. 3:8}

Looking at our present state as a people and nation truly the ability of man to keep themselves and the earth from constant decline is ever so visible. Undoubtedly, the arms of FLESH have failed us and we are reaping the curse of it as the scriptures says. Too long have we placed the responsibilities of a spiritual battle into the hands of carnal men. To release our lands and their people from the desolation that has come upon them a new order must be enacted. We, the believers, must begin to lift up the standard of the Lord by reinstituting the demonstrated power of God into our sin sick regions to destroy the works of the devil that the natural order of God may be reestablished.

RESTORING REGIONS REVIEWS

The Restoring Regions Training Manual is very easy to read. If the practical but biblically supported instructions in this manual are applied by those in hopes of restoring regions from negative forces and strongholds then, this manual will help to ensure the reader and his/her team to be combative victoriously over those opposing regions. This manual definitely empowers the reader to fight the good fight of faith in hopes of restoration!

James Larimore, Pastor
Open Door of Faith Ministries
Conway, South Carolina

In his, Restoring Regions Manual, Apostle Gaskins has done an outstanding job of introducing and acquainting both youth and adults alike; with the necessary knowledge and tools to effectively take back spiritually what naturally belongs to the saints. Apostle Gaskins has indeed presented powerful spiritual truths with great simplicity and clarity. He uses dynamic Bible principles along with scriptures that are extremely practical, relevant, and readily applicable. I highly recommend this manual for all leaders and believers that are ready to strategically storm the enemies camp.

Apostle Catlin Williams, Sr.
Pastor, Shabach Tabernacle of Worship
Bishop, Chosen Assembly of Christ, Inc.
Philadelphia, Pa.

The anointing of God is clearly evident in Apostle Detrick L. Gaskins as ministered with deep and dynamic revelation in this book "Restoring Regions Training Manual" I strong recommend this book to all Men and Women of God and especially to all missionary Pastor and Apostles of God. This book will give you clear and complete understanding how to expand the king of God by operating affectively in called region. This book will help you to learn and under fundamental of the ministry and division of every gift and calling. And also will teach you that how to make strategies to be successful in the ministry.

Apostle Christee
Founder & Chairman
Back to Jesus Ministries International
Lahore, Pakistan.

RESTORING REGIONS is a clarion call to the body of Christ, a book that I recommend to every born-again believer, especially to every 5-fold leader. The time has come that we take the Kingdom of God by force, taking back everything that belongs to us. It is time for us to advance the Kingdom of God by making Christ name known in the earth. Acts 3: 20-21 tell us, "And he shall send Jesus Christ, which before was preached unto you: Whom the heaven must receive until the times of restitution of all things, which God hath spoken by the mouth of all his holy prophets since the world began". This is a season where I believe God is restoring all things, especially the 5 fold ministry so that we can restore regions and that Christ's bride will be ready for His triumphant return. Before Christ returns we understand that end-time revival and reformation must happen, which is quickly approaching us. This book will prepare us for such movement.

Pastor Derrick C. Parker,
Senior Leader God's House Church and Ministries
Baltimore, Maryland

RESTORING REGIONS
POST THOUGHT

The Church in its differing gifts and functions can glean expounding insight and strategy for implementation from the author's content. For readers needing advanced methods of information in an easy to read format, the writing is supportive and appropriate for all levels of ministry for youth leaders, musicians, missionaries, pastors, apostles, prophets, scribes and the equipping of all church members and leadership with the intent to restore regionally what belongs to the believers. The author, Apostle Detrick Gaskins uses a power point approach in the writing that can simulate and stimulate group training for quick references and team building targeting specific sections of focus. I believe this format of presentation is vital in the 21st Century Church. We are now living in the information age and the crave to access vital information quickly is met by the style in which the book is written. *Restoring Regions* gives sound scriptural references that are not simply opinion based but that are doctrinally sound. The manual is enabled with insights necessary for focus and agenda organizing.

Anthony J. Wells,
Apostolic and Prophetic Leader
Oasis House of Destiny Intl,
Nashville, Tn.

Study Tools

Aol Research and Learn Dictionary

Studylight.org

Webster's New World Dictionary

KJV Parallel Bible

King James Bible Commentary

Strong's Exhaustive Concordance of the Bible

Nelson's Illustrated Bible Dictionary

Holman Bible Dictionary

Wikipedia

"Restoring Regions"

Apostle Detrick L. Gaskins